Inspired Recipes from Nebraska

© 2008 Friends of the Governor's Residence.
All rights reserved.

Except for brief quotes used in reviews, no part of this book may be reproduced, stored in a retrieval system, or transmitted in any form by any means, including mechanical, electronic, photocopying, recording, or otherwise, without prior written permission of the copyright holder.

Infusionmedia Publishing Inc.
140 North 8th Street
205 The Apothecary
Lincoln, NE 68508-1358
www.infusionmediapublishing.com

Printed in the U.S.A.

10 9 8 7 6 5 4 3 2 1
First Edition

ISBN: 978-0-9796586-5-5

Library of Congress Control Number: 2008931880

Historical photographs of the Governor's Residence are provided by the Nebraska State Historical Society.

Recent photos of the Residence and Kathy Henning are provided by Sam Fifer, Office of the Chief Information Officer for the State of Nebraska.

The Heineman-Ganem family photograph on page one is by David Dale/www.daviddalephoto.com.

Contents

v
Welcome
Sally Ganem

1
Governor & First Lady Recipes

13
Appetizers & Beverages

43
Breads & Rolls

79
Soups, Salads & Vegetables

121
Main Dishes & Casseroles

167
Meat, Poultry & Seafood

211
Pies, Pastries & Desserts

257
Cakes, Cookies & Candy

297
This & That

313
Complete Meals

347
Acknowledgements

350
Index

The custom carpet in the foyer entrance of the Residence is full of Nebraska symbols: the sower, cottonwood, goldenrod, meadowlark, white-tailed deer, honey bee, blue agate, and corn.

Welcome

In 1958, the current Governor's Residence was officially completed and an open house was held for the public. Over the years this home has hosted dignitaries and numerous public activities, making it live up to its image of the "people's house." This book provides a glimpse of the rich history of the Governor's Residence, as well as our heritage as a State through the stories that accompany many of the recipes.

Governor Dave Heineman, Sam, and I invite you to sample these wonderful recipes that have been submitted from across the state. "Nebraska, the Good Life" is what has "inspired recipes from Nebraska."

Enjoy!

Sally Ganem

Sally Ganem
First Lady of the State of Nebraska

Dave Heineman
Governor

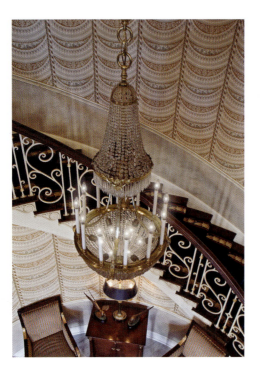

The crystal chandelier that hangs in the entrance is actually two chandeliers made into one.

On each step of the curved stairway that leads to the private quarters you will find the symbol of a pineapple, representing hospitality and friendship. According to legend, the pineapple on the ninth step is left unfinished to ward off evil spirits.

Originally, Nebraska governors provided their own living accommodations. Then in 1899, $25,000 was appropriated to purchase and furnish a governor's residence. An existing house was purchased that was located on a block next to the current Residence—an elegant house that included a ballroom on the third floor.

The current Governor's Residence building was started in 1957 and opened in 1958. It is a modified Georgian Colonial with thirty-one rooms, five bedrooms, twelve bathrooms, four fireplaces, and a three-stall garage. Governor Victor E. Anderson, the twenty-ninth governor of the state, was the first governor to live in the current Residence.

Governor & First Lady Recipes

Dave Heineman (center), the thirty-ninth governor of Nebraska, First Lady Sally Ganem (right), and their son Sam in the Governor's Residence.

The ornate doorknobs were saved from the first Residence and used for the interior doors of the Residence entry

In April 1997, First Lady Diane Nelson announced that forty years of wear and tear had made the house pretty shabby, and a fundraising project to restore it to its original elegance was initiated. The home was remodeled from top to bottom.

In August 2007, the Governor and First Lady unveiled the etchings of the Nebraska State Quarter on the doors in the Office of the Residence. Funding was provided by the community of Hartington.

Stuffed Grape Leaves

1 cup of washed rice
Salt, to taste
Cinnamon, about 1/4 to 1/2 teaspoon
Black pepper, to taste
Dash of nutmeg
1 to 1 1/2 pounds of hamburger or ground lamb

Place rice in a pan. Add salt. Add cinnamon. Add black pepper. Add nutmeg. Mix with your hands. Add hamburger or ground lamb.

Jars of grape leaves can be purchased in most major grocery stores. Wash the leaves with water since they come in salt brine. Otherwise, fresh leaves picked from a wild grape vine will need to be dipped in boiling water to make them pliable to roll.

Line the bottom of a pan with a layer of grape leaves.

Unroll each leaf and put about a teaspoon of the rice mixture at one end of the leaf and roll halfway, stopping to fold in the sides of the leaf, and continue to roll, placing it seam side down in the pan.

Continue with each leaf until all are rolled and placed in the pan. There will be more than one layer and they can be stacked on top of each other.

There are two versions for different tastes:

Lemon Base

Fill the pan with juice of 1 lemon and water to cover the grape leaves. Add a

You may notice that specific amounts of spices are not given—it depends on the taste of the cook!

Governor & First Lady Recipes

little salt to the water if using fresh leaves. Place an inverted plate on top of the leaves to prevent unrolling and cover the pan with a lid. Bring to a boil and simmer for about 30 to 45 minutes, or until the rice is done.

Tomato Base

Fill the pan with 1 can of tomato paste (6 ounces) mixed with enough water to cover the leaves. Place an inverted plate on top of the leaves to prevent unrolling, and cover the pan with a lid. Bring to a boil, and simmer for about 30 to 45 minutes, or until the rice is done.

Variations:

Cabbage Rolls

Core the cabbage. Separate cabbage leaves. Dip leaves in boiling water to make them pliable to roll. Fill and roll as described in the directions for the grape leaves. Roll them tight. Cover the bottom of the pan with cabbage leaves and a clove of garlic. Set rolls in the pan. Sprinkle with salt. Mix 1 can of tomato paste (6 ounces) with enough hot water to cover the leaves. Bring to a boil. Reduce heat to simmer and cook for about an hour.

Squash

Core the centers of yellow summer squash. Fill about three-quarters full with rice stuffing mixture, as rice will expand. Bake at 350° for 20 to 25 minutes, or until tender.

Do you have leftover rice stuffing mixture? Form into small balls and drop in with the leaves and you have porcupine meatballs. Enjoy!

First Lady Sally Ganem

Tabbouleh

1 cup of bulgur (cracked wheat, which can be purchased at most major grocery stores)
Cover the bulgur with boiling water and let soak for about 5 minutes. Drain and press out excess water.

1 cup finely chopped onion
Mix with the bulgur, crushing the onion juice into the cracked wheat with your fingers.

Salt and pepper, add to taste (freshly ground black pepper is great in this recipe)

Add to the bulgur mixture:

1 1/2 cups chopped parsley
1 Tablespoon of dried mint (if using fresh mint, add about 1/2 cup)
1 or 2 tomatoes, seeded and chopped
Olive oil, about 1/2 cup
1 cup of lemon juice (use real lemons)

Mix and taste for seasoning. Place on a large platter and garnish. I use sprigs of parsley and grape tomatoes. You can decorate with quartered tomatoes or otherwise garnish the dish however you wish.

First Lady Sally Ganem

These recipes came from my grandparents who emigrated from Lebanon to America in the early 1900s, making Nebraska their home and becoming Americans to have freedom and a better way of life—as did many immigrants from many countries from this period. We serve these dishes at our yearly family reunion.

Sally's Favorite Salad Dressing

8 cups of mixed salad greens
   or **1/2 head of romaine and 1/2 head of iceberg lettuce, chopped**
1 large lemon
1/4 cup olive oil
1/2 teaspoon garlic powder
1/4 teaspoon salt
1/4 teaspoon black pepper
1/4 cup dried mint leaves
1 small red onion, chopped

Put salad greens in large salad bowl. Squeeze lemon over greens. Drizzle with olive oil and seasonings. Add red onion, toss, and serve!

First Lady Sally Ganem

Much of the furniture found in the formal dining room of the Governor's Residence was either purchased for or donated to the Residence and was refinished or reupholstered during the 1997 renovation.

Green Beans with a Mediterranean Twist

Sauté 1 thinly sliced onion in 1/2 cup oil

Add about 2 pounds of string beans, cleaned and trimmed (you may slice them to whichever size you want or keep them whole)

Add a little salt, about 1/2 to 1 teaspoon

Add a dash of nutmeg

Add black pepper, about 1/2 teaspoon

Add about 1 teaspoon of cinnamon

Combine 1 small can of tomato paste (6 ounces) with water, enough to cover the beans.

Cover the pan and bring to a boil. Reduce heat to simmer and cook slowly until the beans are done, about an hour.

First Lady Sally Ganem

The demi-lunes (see the photo on page 44) on either side of the fireplace were hand-painted by Nebraska artist Andy Moore.

Middle Eastern Lemonade

1 lemon
Sugar to taste
Cold water
Few drops orange-blossom water
Ice cubes
Mint sprig

Squeeze lemon into a tall glass. Add sugar to taste. Fill with cold water. Add orange-blossom water and ice cubes. Stir. Garnish with mint sprig.

Makes 1 serving.

Variations:

Use store-bought lemonade and add a few drops of orange-blossom water to your glass.

Use club soda instead of water in the recipe for a lemon fizz.

First Lady Sally Ganem

The 'Gov' Burger

1 1/2 pounds lean ground beef (85% lean ground beef recommended)
1 teaspoon Misty's Natural All Purpose Seasoning
1/2 teaspoon salt
1/2 teaspoon pepper
4 slices cheese (from the UNL Dairy Store)
8 slices fully cooked bacon
4 whole-wheat hamburger buns

Optional: Garnish with romaine lettuce leaves and tomato slices.

Combine ground beef, Misty's seasoning, salt, and pepper in large bowl, mixing lightly but thoroughly. Lightly shape into 4 3/4-inch thick patties. Place patties on grill. Cook over medium heat, uncovered, for 13 to 15 minutes to medium (160˚) doneness, until no longer pink in the center and juices show no pink color, turning once.

To melt cheese on patties, place a cheese slice on each patty for 1 minute before patties are done.

Place burger on bun and top with 2 fully cooked bacon slices.

Makes 4 servings.

Governor Dave Heineman

A Heineman family favorite!

Creamed Corn

18 cups corn, cut from the cob
1 pound butter
1 pint half-and-half

Preheat oven to 325°. Put all ingredients into a roaster. Do NOT cover. Bake for 1 hour, stirring occasionally. Cool. Freeze in 2-cup containers or freezer bags.

Irene Heineman, mother of Governor Dave Heineman

The remodeling of the Governor's Residence begun in April 1997 included structural changes which needed to be made—ADA accessibility (including an elevator), smoke-detection equipment and a sprinkler system, new wiring and lighting, new windows, air-flow modifications, asbestos removal, and updated security equipment. It took eighteen months to complete the renovation. The building was reopened to the public in August 1998.

The antique Spanish oak paneling in the Residence Office was saved and restored from the foyer of the original residence.

The built-in cabinetry in the Residence Office incorporates carvings of ears of corn as a reflection of Nebraska's heritage.

Governor & First Lady Recipes

The original Front Foyer.

Appetizers & Beverages

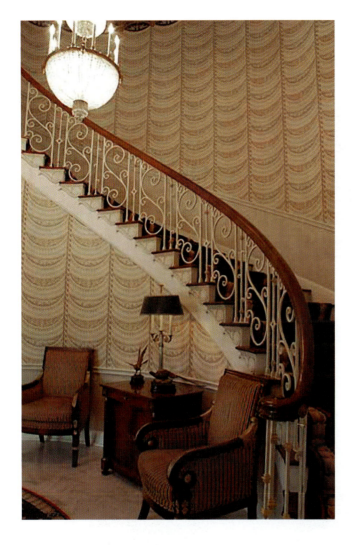

The Front Foyer

As you enter the Governor's Residence, a staircase leads to the second floor. The residence features thirty-one rooms, four fireplaces, and a three-stall garage. Governor Victor Anderson was the first governor to live in the Residence.

The grand piano is one of two pieces of furniture saved from the first Governor's Residence.

The empire sofa that is featured in the formal drawing room is the second piece that was saved from the first Governor's Residence.

Appetizers & Beverages

Baked Gizzards

5 pounds gizzards
1 teaspoon salt
1/2 teaspoon pepper
2 teaspoons garlic powder
1/2 cup chopped onion
1 1/2 sticks margarine

Gizzards should be thawed, rinsed, and drained. In a Dutch oven, melt margarine. Add salt, pepper, garlic powder, and onion. Add gizzards, stir to cover with mixture, and bake 3 hours at 300°. Place in Crock-Pot to keep warm.

Lieutenant Governor Rick Sheehy

This is a favorite of our family.

In the formal dining room, the empire sofa and grand piano are the only pieces from the first Governor's Residence. The rest of the furniture was either donated to the Nebraska State Historical Society or sold at public auction when the new house was built.

Appetizers & Beverages

Crabmeat Mold

3 cans crabmeat
1 cup Miracle Whip
1 cup half-and-half
1 envelope Knox Original Unflavored Gelatin
1 teaspoon chopped green onion or chives
2 teaspoons Worcestershire sauce
1/4 teaspoon white pepper
1/4 teaspoon lemon juice

Heat half-and-half and add gelatin. Stir until dissolved. Remove from heat, add rest of ingredients, and pour into mold sprayed with Pam Cooking Spray. Chill.

Bill Orr, Former First Gentleman

Mom's Yummy Cheese Ball

This is a real hit for my family at Christmas gatherings.

2 (8-ounce) packages cream cheese
1 cup mild cheddar cheese, shredded
1/4 cup chopped onion
2 cups chopped pecans
1 (8-ounce) can crushed pineapple, drained

Reserve 1 cup pecans. Mix remaining ingredients and form into a ball. Roll in pecans. Make 1 large or 2 small balls. Store in refrigerator.

Alice Dubbs

Appetizers & Beverages

Cheese Crisps

1/2 cup butter
2 cups cheddar cheese (soft)
1/2 teaspoon salt
1/8 teaspoon cayenne
1 cup Rice Krispies, crushed
1 cup sifted flour

Shape into cookies and bake at 375° about 12 minutes. Can freeze and reheat.

Senator DiAnna Schimek

German Cheese Spread

1 stick butter (no substitutes)
1 (8-ounce) package cream cheese (softened)

Add:

2 to 3 green onions, finely chopped, can include tops
1 Tablespoon Hungarian paprika (heaping)

Mix together. Should be a nice salmon color; if too light, add more paprika, 1 teaspoon at a time. Chill. Can be garnished with capers. Serve with cocktail rye bread or Wheat Thins.

Senator Pat Engel

This recipe came from my mother, Elizabeth Wilmot Rebman, granddaughter of Albert Hoyt Byrum, who served in the Nebraska Legislature in the early 1900s. He was a member of the Constitutional Convention from 1920–1921

We lived in Weisbaden, Germany, in the late '50s where I was stationed with the Air Force. Dee and I would sometimes eat at a nearby Bierstub. They would bring this cheese spread to the table, served with thin slices of dark pumpernickel rye bread. It was delicious and Dee asked for the recipe. They didn't speak English and our German wasn't great, so they took her to the kitchen and showed her!

Appetizers & Beverages

Beef and Cheese Ball

24 ounces cream cheese
6 ounces chopped beef
1 bunch green onions, chopped
1 Tablespoon Worcestershire sauce
1 Tablespoon Ac'cent (monosodium glutamate or MSG)

Soften cream cheese and mix together with other ingredients. Shape into a ball. Refrigerate overnight. This makes an attractive cheese ball for Christmas.

Kristi Leckband

Wood carving throughout the Residence was done by Keats Lorenz, who also carved the Senate Chamber door in the Capitol. Much of the artwork throughout the Residence is on loan from the Joslyn Art Museum, Sheldon Memorial Art Gallery, and the Nebraska State Historical Society.

Cowboy Caviar

1 can pinto beans, drained
1 can black eye peas, drained
1 small can diced chilies, drained
1 can white corn, drained
2 stalks celery, chopped
1/2 red onion, chopped
1 green pepper, chopped
2 to 3 roma tomatoes, chopped

Put in bowl with above:

1/2 cup vinegar
1/2 cup oil
1/2 cup sugar
1 teaspoon salt
1 teaspoon pepper

Boil these ingredients for 30 seconds to a minute. Let cool completely, then pour over top of mixture. Refrigerate overnight. Serve with Fritos Scoops.

Perky Weatherly

Reuben Balls

5 ounces dried beef
1 cup Cheez-It cheese cracker crumbs, divided
1 (8-ounce) package cream cheese
1 Tablespoon finely chopped onion
1 (10-ounce) can sauerkraut, well drained
Milk

Snip dried beef pieces. Mix with 1/4 cup crumbs. Soften cream cheese with onion. Chop sauerkraut; add to beef mixture. Form balls, dip into milk, roll in remaining cracker crumbs. Place on greased baked sheet. Bake at 350° for 15 minutes.

Makes 2 dozen.

Laurie Schepmann

Garlic Dip

Philadelphia Cream Cheese (room temperature)
Worcestershire sauce
Heinz Tomato Ketchup
Garlic powder
Garlic Salt
Sour cream (add to thickness desired)

Peggy Green

My mother, Elna Green, loved to collect recipes and cookbooks, but I seldom saw her use one. She prepared most recipes by memory or taste. When I started entertaining my friends, I wanted to impress them with this great dip. I asked her for the recipe and she gave me a handwritten recipe card with six ingredients, no measurements. To this day, I still can't make it taste as good as my mother's blend.

The architect of the Governor's Residence, begun in 1957, was Selmer Solehim & Associates. The building was 15,340 square feet.

Appetizers & Beverages

Scooper Beef

3 pounds lean ground beef or ground round
1 package taco seasoning with 1/2 cup water
2 (8-ounce) packages cream cheese
1/4 cup milk
4 tablespoons mild green chilies, diced
4 medium tomatoes, peeled, seeded, chopped, and drained
1 cup green onion, finely chopped
1 1/2 cups lettuce, finely chopped
1 (8-ounce) bottle mild taco sauce
8 ounces cheddar cheese, shredded

Brown ground beef and drain. Add taco seasoning with water to beef and simmer 15 minutes. Set aside to cool. Mix cream cheese and milk with mixer until creamy. Spread on a 13-inch round serving plate, leaving a small rim and making it look like a pie shell. Spread beef (when cool) over cream cheese crust, saving 1/2 cup beef. Sprinkle green chilies over beef. Add a layer of tomatoes, next a layer of onions, and then a layer of lettuce. Sprinkle taco sauce over top. Add cheddar cheese overall. Top with the remaining 1/2 cup beef. Serve at once or can be chilled. It is best served within a few hours of preparation, as it tends to get watery overnight. Serve with chips or crackers.

Kathy Graham, Administrative Assistant to Governor Dave Heineman

Chicken Enchilada Dip

A potluck favorite at Creighton University!

1 (8-ounce) package cream cheese
2 cups Mexican-style shredded cheese (do not use taco cheese)
1 small can chopped green chilies, not drained
1 teaspoon garlic powder
1/4 teaspoon chili powder
1 pound boneless, skinless chicken breast, cooked and shredded or
    drained, shredded canned chicken breast
1 (8-ounce) jar of mayonnaise (do not use Miracle Whip)
Chopped jalapeño, to taste

Add all ingredients to a small Crock-Pot and heat until cheeses are melted.
You may garnish with chopped tomatoes, green peppers, or green onions.
Serve with tortilla chips or party bread.

Carol Lewis

Sunflower Seed Dip

2 cups bottled ranch-style salad dressing
1 (10-ounce) package frozen chopped spinach, thawed, well drained
1 cup sour cream
1 cup unsalted, shelled sunflower seeds
2 green onions, thinly sliced
1/4 cup diced celery
1 (2-ounce) jar diced pimiento, drained

Mix well. Refrigerate covered at least 1 hour to let flavors blend. Serve with raw vegetables or crackers.

Jayne Schram

The First Ladies' and Gentleman's Hall features the portraits of Nebraska's First Ladies and one First Gentleman, Bill Orr. Mrs. Charles Bryan started the collection in 1932.

Marinated Eggplant, Italian Melanzane Marinate

1 medium eggplant
1 cup olive oil
1/4 cup wine vinegar
1/4 cup parsley, chopped
1/2 cup green olives with pimiento, chopped
2 garlic cloves, quartered
Red pepper, to taste
Oregano, to taste

Peel whole eggplant. Slice paper thin. Put in layer on layer in colander, sprinkling salt between layers. Leave overnight in refrigerator to remove water from eggplant. Set colander on bowl to catch water drippings.

Mix the remaining ingredients together in a bowl. Place sliced eggplant in jar or bowl and sprinkle the marinade on each layer. The longer the above process is stored in refrigerator, the more flavor will be achieved.

Lou Turco, Acela Turco

The Honorable Order of the Golden Toque is the highest acclaimed recognition a chef may receive in America. To qualify, chefs must have twenty years' experience and have achieved high professional standing and distinguished service in the culinary profession and arts. Chefs must be nominated by at least two members in good standing. It takes an average of three years to get through the qualification process. Membership is restricted to only 100 lifetime members. At one time, Omaha had five Golden Toque members, the only city with more than two members. Chefs included: Al Buda, Blackstone Hotel; Richard Bolamperti, Louie Cantoni's Restaurant; Joe Incontro, Chieftan Hotel, Indian Hills Restaurant; Lou Turco, **continued on page 26**

continued from page 25

The Townhouse; Paul Goebel, Holiday Inn and later The New Tower Inn. Joe Villella, from the Rome Hotel, was also inducted as an Honorary.

Garlic Marinated Mushrooms

1 pound fresh mushrooms
1/3 cup vinegar
2 Tablespoons water
1/2 to 3/4 cup olive oil
1 package Italian seasoning mix
1 large garlic clove, minced

Put the mushrooms in a jar. Add all ingredients and marinate overnight in refrigerator.

Frank Chilese

English Olive Appetizers

1 cup shredded sharp cheddar cheese
1 1/2 cups (8-ounce can) minced black olives
1 cup mayonnaise
1 medium onion, chopped
1/2 teaspoon curry powder
6 English muffins

Combine shredded cheese, olives, mayonnaise, onion, and curry powder. Spread mixture on English muffin halves. Cut each into 4 wedges. Place on a cookie sheet and bake at 350° for about 10 minutes or until golden brown.

Peggy Green

Appetizers & Beverages

Mushroom Croustades

36 3-inch circles of bread
5 Tablespoons butter
4 Tablespoons minced onion
1/2 pound minced mushrooms
2 Tablespoons flour
1 cup half-and-half
1/2 teaspoon salt
1/8 teaspoon cayenne pepper
1/4 teaspoon black pepper
1 1/2 Tablespoons chopped dehydrated chives
2 Tablespoons parsley
1 teaspoon lemon juice
Parmesan cheese, grated

Cut 36 circles of bread with a 3-inch cutter. Spread one side with butter and fit buttered side down inside of tiny muffin tins, pushing center to make a cup. Bake at 400° for 10 minutes or until lightly browned. Remove and cool. Can be frozen at this point.

Filling

Cook onions in butter; add mushrooms and stir for 10 to 15 minutes until moisture evaporates. Remove from heat and sprinkle with flour and mix. Pour in half-and-half, return to heat, and bring to boil. Cook until thick. Remove from heat then add spices and lemon juice. Cool. Fill bread cups and top with a sprinkle of Parmesan cheese. Can be frozen after being filled. Sprinkle with Parmesan cheese just before baking. Bake 350° for 15 minutes.

Lori Pankonin

A great do-ahead appetizer for any type of crowd. It is the old reliable that I always include when I am being adventurous and trying other new recipes on my guests!

Appetizers & Beverages

This is a recipe my neighbor Wilma and I created for my daughter's graduation party. She wanted something different to serve. At the time, we made 600 potatoes. It's something friends and family request.

Stuffed Baby Baked Potatoes

12 small (1 1/2- to 2-inch) new round, red potatoes
1/2 cup sour cream
1/2 cup shredded cheddar cheese
1/2 cup chopped crispy fried bacon
1/2 cup minced fresh chives (.05-ounce container = 1/4 cup)

Preheat oven to 35°. Scrub potatoes and leave skins on. Dry completely. Prick with a fork and place on baking pan. Bake 30 to 40 minutes or until tender. When done, cool potatoes slightly. Cut potatoes in half. Using a small melon baller, remove pulp from center of each half. Mix sour cream, cheese, bacon, and chives together and scoop back into potatoes. May sprinkle with a bit of shredded cheese. Warm in oven until ready to serve.

Nancy Enstrom, Wilma L. Lorenz

In the First Ladies' and Gentleman's Hall, there was no portrait of Mrs. Ezra P. Savage for many years because she was very superstitious and did not permit pictures. However, the portrait of her standing on the USS Nebraska was sent to the Residence in 1972.

Appetizers & Beverages

Hanky Panky

1 pound lean ground beef
1 pound whole-hog pork sausage
1 pound processed cheese spread (Velveeta)
1 teaspoon Worcestershire sauce
1 teaspoon oregano
1 teaspoon minced garlic
1 Tablespoon chopped onion
2 loaves cocktail rye bread

Brown and crumble meats; drain. Add cheese, Worcestershire sauce, oregano, garlic, and onion; stir over low heat just until cheese is melted. Spread mixture on rye bread squares. Place on cookie sheet and broil until cheese is lightly browned (only takes 2 or 3 minutes).

Serves 12.

Ninajean Rohlfs

These may be frozen in layers with waxed paper between and taken out to broil a few at a time. Hanky Panky makes a nice appetizer, a tasty snack, an accompaniment to soup, or can be served with scrambled eggs for breakfast ... basically good anytime! These favorite snacks have an unusual name. We had an old bachelor neighbor who often "just happened to stop by" near supper-time. One time he was a little too late, so Mom just made us all a snack from the stash she kept in the freezer. When it was done, she hollered out the door, "Come on in, guys, for some hanky panky." Our neighbor turned red, mumbled an excuse, and took off in a hurry!

Appetizers & Beverages

This is a copycat recipe from my favorite Italian restaurant.

Tomato and Basil Appetizer

6 Tablespoons virgin olive oil
6 roma tomatoes, chopped fine
1 1/2 teaspoons onion, chopped fine
2 to 3 stems fresh basil, chopped fine

Mix all ingredients and refrigerate several hours. Serve on slices of your favorite French bread.

Senator Gail Kopplin

Cranberry Roll-Ups

8 ounces cream cheese
1/4 cup crushed pineapple, drained
1/3 cup dried cranberries
2 Tablespoon chopped jalapeño pepper
2 Tablespoon sugar
1/4 cup chopped pecans

Mix first 6 ingredients. Divide equally and spread on 3 tortillas. Wrap in plastic wrap. Refrigerate for several hours. Unwrap and cut into 1-inch slices.

Nadine Anderson

Caramel Apple Cones

This appetizer took First Place in Nebraska City.

6 small Nebraska City Golden Delicious apples
1 (14-ounce) package of caramels (about 50)
2 teaspoons water
6 waffle cones or sugar ice cream cones
3/4 pound of melting chocolate
1/2 cup peanut butter
1/2 cup powdered sugar
16 ounces white melting chocolate

Core, wash, and dry apples. Melt caramel and water over medium-low heat until completely melted. Dip apples and set on greased wax paper. Refrigerate for 1 hour.

Coat the inside of cones with melted chocolate. Mix peanut butter and powdered sugar. Distribute peanut-butter mixture evenly in cones and top with more melted chocolate. Place apples in cones and dip tops in melted chocolate. When chocolate is dry, spoon melted white chocolate over tops of apples and refrigerate. Then enjoy!

Robyn Gay

Appetizers & Beverages

Spiced Candied Walnuts

Peanut or canola oil
4 cups walnut halves
1 cup confectioner's sugar, sifted
1/2 teaspoon cayenne pepper
1/2 teaspoon ground cinnamon
Pinch of salt, or more to taste
1/4 teaspoon freshly ground black pepper

In a large, heavy-bottomed skillet, heat about 1 inch of oil to 350°. Bring a large pot of water to boil. Add walnuts and blanch for 30 seconds. Drain and transfer nuts to a medium bowl. While nuts are still hot and slightly wet, add confectioner's sugar and toss to coat nuts. Stir and toss until all the sugar has melted into the nuts; if bits of unmelted sugar remain on nuts, they will not fry properly. Stir nuts again before frying. Using a large slotted spoon, transfer a few nuts to the hot oil, allowing the foam to subside before adding another spoonful. (Otherwise, oil could foam over and burn you.) Fry in small batches until nuts are medium brown, about 45 seconds per batch; be careful not to overcook. Scatter on unlined baking sheet to cool slightly. In a small bowl, stir together cayenne, cinnamon, salt, and pepper. While nuts are still warm, transfer them to a bowl and sprinkle evenly with about half of spice mix. Toss well to distribute spices and then taste a nut. Add more spice mix, to taste, and toss well after each addition. When cool, pack in airtight jar. They will keep at room temperature for at least 2 weeks.

Senator Pete Pirsch

Appetizers & Beverages

Sugared Pecans

1 pound pecans
1 Tablespoon water
1 egg white
1 cup sugar
1 teaspoon salt
2 teaspoons cinnamon

Beat water and egg in large bowl until frothy. Pour in the pecans and stir until totally covered. In another bowl, combine the sugar, cinnamon, and salt. Pour in pecans and stir until all the nuts are covered. Spread the pecans on a baking sheet and cook at 250° for 45 to 60 minutes, stirring every 15 minutes.

Senator Annette Dubas

Nebraska became the thirty-seventh state in 1867, and the First Ladies' and Gentleman's Hall contains portraits of the six Territorial Governors.

Vodka and Citrus Cured Salmon

2 pound salmon fillet, with skin
1/2 cup kosher salt
3 Tablespoons sugar
1/4 cup chopped fresh dill
1/4 cup lemon-flavored vodka
2 Tablespoons grated lemon zest
2 Tablespoons grated lime zest
2 Tablespoons grated orange zest

Rinse salmon under cold water and pat dry. Place salmon, skin side down, on several large sheets of plastic wrap. Mix salt, sugar, dill, vodka, and all the zests. Spread mixture evenly over fleshy side of fish, pressing into the flesh. Wrap salmon tightly in plastic wrap and place skin side down in large baking dish. Place ceramic dish on top of salmon and weight dish with heavy cans. Refrigerate 24 to 48 hours. Unwrap salmon and rinse the cure off under cold, running water. Pat dry and slice diagonally into paper-thin slices.

Becki Wiechman

Best Holiday Fish

4 to 5 ounces of fresh smoked salmon
1 (12-ounce) package of cream cheese
1 Tablespoon lemon juice
2 teaspoons grated onion
1 Tablespoon horseradish
1/4 teaspoon salt
4 teaspoons liquid smoke

Combine all ingredients into softened cream cheese. Shred the salmon into small pieces and mix into the cream cheese mixture. Can be made into a ball or log rolled in nuts or parsley. This is best if cooled overnight. Serve with your favorite kind of crackers.

Senator Gail Kopplin

This is a special-events appetizer that has been passed down through the family.

Poor Man's Cappuccino Mix

1 cup instant coffee creamer
1 cup chocolate drink mix (Nesquik, formerly called Nestlé Quik)
2/3 cup instant coffee crystals
1/2 cup sugar
1/2 teaspoon ground cinnamon
1/2 teaspoon ground nutmeg

Combine all ingredients and mix well. Makes 3 cups of dry mix. Mix 3 tablespoons with 6 to 8 ounces hot water. This can also be topped with shredded chocolate or whipped cream.

Senator Gail Kopplin

Summer Punch

2 packages strawberry Kool-Aid
1 (6-ounce) can pineapple juice
1 (6-ounce) can frozen orange juice
2 bottles club soda (regular drinking size)
1 large bottle ginger ale
6 to 8 cups water
1 cup sugar

Mix all ingredients in large bowl and serve over ice or freeze to slush stage and serve. Makes about 20 cups.

Bonnie Burling

Kool-Aid was invented around 1927 by Edwin Perkins and his wife Kitty in Hastings. The couple were running a mail-order business and one of their bestsellers was a drink syrup called Fruit Smack. In an effort to cut shipping costs, Perkins got rid of the four-ounce glass bottles that Fruit Smack syrup was sold in and instead packaged it as a concentrated powder in an envelope. Kool-Aid was born.

Appetizers & Beverages

Cranberry-Apple Punch

64 ounces cranberry juice cocktail
32 ounces apple juice
4 Tablespoons lemon juice
1 cup brown sugar
4 sticks cinnamon, broken into pieces
2 teaspoons allspice
2 teaspoons whole cloves
Orange slices

Pour juices in a large pot. Add sugar and stir until dissolved. Place cinnamon, allspice, and cloves in a piece of cheesecloth and put in pot of juices. Cook on low for 2 hours. Add orange slices. Serve.

Julie Sheppard

Mock Champagne

1 cup sugar
1 cup water
2 1/4 cups grapefruit juice
1 cup orange juice
3/4 cup grenadine syrup
2 quarts gingerale

Combine sugar and water in saucepan. Bring to a boil, stirring frequently. Remove from heat. Cool slightly. Add juices and grenadine syrup; mix well. Chill until serving time. Add ginger ale just before serving.

Makes 16 servings.

Jane Oligmueller

This sweet tea was a highlight at Chi Omega Executive Headquarters in Memphis, Tennessee, where I worked following college graduation. I served it at my bridal luncheon in Fremont and continue to use the recipe when I entertain here in Chicago.

Sweet Almond Tea

10 cups water divided (8 cups, 2 cups)
2 cups boiling water, in addition to above
1 cup sugar
2 large family-sized tea bags
1 (12-ounce) can of frozen lemonade concentrate, thawed
1 Tablespoon vanilla extract
1 Tablespoon almond extract

To make sugar, combine 2 cups of water and the sugar. Cook and stir until sugar is dissolved. Set aside.

In a 4-quart container, pour the 2 cups of boiling water over the tea bags. Let stand for 5 minutes then remove the tea bags. Add the remaining 8 cups of water, sugar syrup, lemonade concentrate, and vanilla and almond extracts. Refrigerate.

Makes 14 (8-ounce) servings.

Lisa Enstrom Glathar

Appetizers & Beverages

Mock Sangria

1 (40-ounce) bottle unsweetened white grape juice, chilled
1 (32-ounce) bottle apple-cranberry juice, chilled
1/2 cup lime juice, chilled
1 (33.8-ounce) bottle club soda, chilled

Garnish

Seedless green grapes
Sliced limes
Sliced oranges

Combine juices. Just before serving, add club soda. Stir and garnish.

Jane Oligmueller

The original Residence Office.

Breads & Rolls

The Residence Office

Used by governors and their spouses over the years, the office on the first floor of the Residence features antique Spanish Oak panelling that was brought from the original governor's mansion. New doors have been added with etchings of the front and back of the Nebraska state quarter.

The demi-lunes that sit on either side of the fireplace in the formal drawing room were handpainted by artist Andy Moore.

This painting in the formal drawing room, *Capitol Seasons,* was created by Omaha artist Allan Tubach and features many of the historic buildings that surround the State Capitol.

Breads & Rolls

Cinnamon Rolls

1 envelope dry yeast dissolved in 1/4 cup warm water
1 egg, beaten
1 cup milk, scaled
2 Tablespoons sugar
2 Tablespoons shortening
1 teaspoon salt
3 1/2 cups flour
1/2 cup sugar
1 1/2 teaspoons cinnamon

Caramel Sauce

1 cup packed brown sugar
3/4 cup butter
1 Tablespoon cream or whole milk

Dissolve yeast in warm water; add egg. Scald the milk and add the sugar, shortening, and salt. When cool, add yeast mixture to milk mixture. Add the flour, cover with wet towel, and let rise until double in size.

Roll out dough to a rectangle and sprinkle it with sugar and cinnamon. Roll up the dough; pressing the edge to seal and slice into 18 to 24 slices.

Make caramel sauce by combining brown sugar, butter, and cream in a saucepan; pour onto ungreased 9 × 13-inch pan. Place rolls on top. Let rise. Bake at 350° for 35 to 40 minutes.

Former First Lady Ruth Thone

These rolls can be covered with a wet towel, refrigerated overnight, and baked the next day.

My father came to this country from Sweden when he was a young boy. My grandparents on my mother's side were also born in Sweden. My recipe represents that heritage.

Swedish Coffee Bread

5 cups flour
1 teaspoon ground cardamom (15 seeds)
1 1/2 cups milk
1/2 cup butter
1/2 cup sugar
1 teaspoon salt
2 eggs (egg plus 1 yolk)
2 packages yeast in 1/4 cup warm water plus 1 teaspoon sugar

Put flour in large bowl and add cardamom. Heat (do not boil) milk and add butter, sugar, and salt. When lukewarm, add 1 egg and 1 yolk (save egg white) using beater. Then add yeast mixture. Add liquids to flour and work with hands until smooth, using up to 3/4 cup flour as needed. If dough no longer sticks to hands, it has been worked enough. Sprinkle with flour, cover with light towel, place in a warm place and let rise and until double in bulk. Make 4 braids or loaves. Cover with towel and let rise until double in bulk. Brush with egg white and sprinkle with sugar and cinnamon. Bake for about 35 minutes or until golden brown at 350°.

Senator Joel T. Johnson

Breads & Rolls

Kolache

Kolach is singular and *kolache* is plural.

1 1/2 Tablespoons yeast
1/2 cup warm water
1/2 Tablespoon sugar
2 cups scalded milk
3/4 cup sugar
2 sticks margarine
4 to 5 egg yolks
1 cup mashed potatoes or 1/2 cup potato flakes
1/2 Tablespoon salt (scant)
5 to 6 cups flour

Combine yeast, 1/2 cup warm water, and 1/2 tablespoon sugar and let soften to activate the yeast. In a large mixing bowl, combine sugar, lukewarm milk, salt, and margarine with 2 cups flour. Beat 2 minutes. Add yeast mixture, egg yolks, and 1 cup flour. Beat 2 minutes. Stir in enough flour to make a soft dough. Knead until soft and elastic. Place in greased bowl. Cover and let rise in a warm, draft-free place until double in bulk, about 1 1/2 hours. Punch dough down; turn onto lightly floured board. Make round buns the size of a walnut or roll dough to about 1/2-inch thick and cut rounds using a juice glass. Place on greased baking sheet at least 2 inches apart. Cover; let rise in warm place until double in size, about 1 hour.

Press an indentation in the center of each bun, leaving a rim 1/4-inch wide. Fill with filling of your choice (see fillings below). Sprinkle each kolach with topping made of 1/3 cup sugar, 1/3 cup flour, 1/2 teaspoon cinnamon, and 1/4 cup margarine. Let rise 10 minutes. Bake in hot oven 400° about 10 to 12 minutes, or until done. Brush kolache with melted margarine.

Verdigre, Nebraska, known as the "Kolach Capitol," is located in the northeast corner of the state next to Verdigris Creek. Verdige is the "Czech Village in the Valley." The little village of 500 people has a proud Czech history, dating back to 1872. On the second full weekend of June every year, Kolach Days, an annual festival is held. The community grows tremendously as visitors come to enjoy such things as Czech meals, polka dances, and a parade. Of course, there are hundreds and hundreds of kolache to be eaten. Verdigre boasts of two buildings on the historical registrar, the ZCBJ Hall and the Community Hotel. The area is also known for its abundance of whitetail deer, wild turkey, and great fishing.
continued on page 48

Breads & Rolls

continued from page 47

Take the drive, enjoy the landscape, come to visit— you will be glad you did!

Remove from baking sheet and cool on wire racks.

Makes about 5 dozen.

Fillings

Apricot Filling
Cook until tender 2 pounds apricots in water to cover. Drain and mash. Add 1 cup sugar.

Prune Filling
Cook 1 pound prunes in water until soft. Drain (save 3 tablespoons), remove pits, grind prunes. Add 1 teaspoon vanilla, 1/4 teaspoon cinnamon, 1/4 cup sugar, and 3 Tablespoons prune juice.

Cottage Cheese Filling
Mash together 1 pound dry cottage cheese, 1 egg yolk, 1/4 cup raisins, 1/4 teaspoon salt, 3/4 sugar. Dust with cinnamon and mix well. Add 1/4 teaspoon vanilla or lemon flavoring.

Delores Ruzicka

Kolace

1 (12-ounce) can evaporated milk (add 2% milk to make 3 cups)
3/4 cup Mazola oil
2 eggs, beaten
3 packages yeast
1/4 cup warm water
1/4 cup sugar
1 Tablespoon salt
5 cups flour
1/2 cup potato flakes

Poppy Seed Filling

1 pound poppy seed
1 1/2 cups milk
2 Tablespoons cream of wheat
Sugar to taste

Streusel Topping

1/4 cup butter
1/4 cup sugar
3/4 cup flour

Mix yeast, warm water (105° to 115°), and sugar together. Let sit awhile to activate yeast.

Add milk, oil, and eggs while whipping. Gradually add salt, flour, and potato flakes to make a dough. Knead the dough until elastic and smooth. Place in a greased bowl. Cover the dough and let rise until double in size. Punch dough

Kolace are a Czech pastry that can be filled with various fruit fillings. My Grandma Ella was a pro at making them. You always knew you could look forward to them on your birthday and every family get-together. My favorite has always been the poppy seed ones.

Breads & Rolls

down; turn onto a lightly floured board. Shape into balls the size of a golf ball. Place on greased baking sheet at least 2 inches apart. Cover; let rise until double in size. Make a small indentation in the center of each bun. Fill with fruit filling of your choice or use poppy seed filling recipe. Top with streusel topping (recipe below). Let rise 10 minutes. Bake at 375° to 400° about 10 to 12 minutes or until done.

For the poppy seed filling, cook the poppy seed, milk, and cream of wheat together. Add sugar to taste.

For the streusel topping, mix butter, sugar, and flour together before sprinkling on top of kolace.

Senator Russ and Jill Karpisek

The first Inaugural Ball at the Governor's Residence was held in 1854. Most of the First Ladies in the First Ladies' and Gentleman's Hall portraits are dressed in their Inaugural Ball gowns.

Breads & Rolls

Kolac Cheese Bread

Sweet dough to cover 9 × 13-inch pan (may use any sweet dough recipe)
4 cups cottage cheese
1/2 cup melted margarine
1 cup sugar
3 eggs
1/2 cup sour cream
Salt, to taste
Pepper, to taste
1/2 teaspoon cinnamon
1 teaspoon vanilla

Topping

1 egg
1/2 cup flour
1/4 cup sugar
1/4 cup milk
Cinnamon
Coconut

Place a layer of sweet dough in a 9 × 13-inch pan. Mix together cottage cheese, margarine, sugar, eggs, sour cream, cinnamon, vanilla, and salt and pepper to taste. Pour on top of the sweet dough. Make a topping of egg, flour, sugar, and milk and pour over cheese filling. Sprinkle with cinnamon and coconut. Bake at 350° for 1 hour.

Senator Annette Dubas

This is a Polish recipe that my father-in-law loves. He always has his sister-in-law make it for Christmas.

Dell Bromm, after moving off the farm, had her family over after church every Sunday. She served this favorite along with many other goodies. She passed away at the age of ninety-three. These rolls are made and served today as the tradition of our family get-together goes on.

Butterscotch Rolls

24 Rhodes Bake-N-Serv Dinner Rolls, thawed but still cold
1 box butterscotch pudding mix, non-instant
1/2 cup pecans, chopped
1/2 cup brown sugar
1/2 cup butter or margarine

Thaw rolls until soft (about 2 hours at room temperature). Spray Bundt pan. Cut dinner rolls in half and dip in dry pudding mix. Arrange rolls in pan and sprinkle with pecans. Sprinkle remaining pudding mix over the top. Combine brown sugar and butter. Heat together until butter is melted and syrup is formed (microwave 1 1/2 minutes). Cool and pour over rolls. Cover with sprayed plastic wrap. Let rise until double in size or even with top of Bundt pan. Carefully remove plastic. Bake at 350° for 30 to 35 minutes. Immediately after baking, loosen from sides of the pan and invert onto a serving dish with 1-inch sides.

Vicki Bromm

Prize Roll Recipe

2 cups shortening
2 cups sugar
4 teaspoons salt
8 eggs
4 packages dry yeast
4 cups warm water
16 cups flour

Combine shortening, sugar, and salt. Add the beaten eggs and blend. Dissolve yeast in a small amount of warm water. Add the warm water and 2 cups flour; mix well. Add the rest of the flour and mix. Knead dough until smooth. Let rise 2 hours. Then make out rolls into desired shapes, let rise, and bake in a 400° oven for 10 minutes.

The dough may be refrigerated and baked at a later time.

Garneta Bauerle

Garneta Bauerle has had over 10,000 cookbooks printed and is known in Imperial for sharing her cooking.

Breads & Rolls

I spent more Saturdays than I can count going to Grandma Pewee's house to help her make these rolls. We would spend the whole day together while we waited for the dough to rise, and the most fun was forming the knots. Her rolls were in such demand by all of the grandkids that we asked her to just give us rolls for our Christmas presents, which she did for many years.

Grandma Pewee's Dinner Rolls

3/4 cup butter-flavored Crisco
3 cups 1% milk
1/2 cup warm water
4 Tablespoons quick-rise yeast
4 cups flour and 6 cups flour
3/4 cup sugar
2 Tablespoons salt
2 eggs

Melt Crisco in a pan. Heat 3 cups milk in a separate pan. Dissolve yeast in 1/2 to 3/4 cup warm water. Pour milk into melted Crisco (125°). Add to yeast mixture. Grease beater. Add 4 cups flour, 3/4 cup sugar, and 2 Tablespoons salt. Mix until smooth. Add the 2 eggs while mixing. Add 6 1/2 (approximate) cups of flour gradually. Knead the dough on a floured board until elastic and smooth. Put into 2 bowls. Grease the tops and let rise until finger indention stays (about 1 hour). Roll dough into baseball-size balls. Roll into about 7-inch strands and then tie into a knot. Let rise. Brush on egg. Sprinkle with sesame seeds and salt. Bake at 325° for 15 minutes or until golden brown. When done, brush with butter and wait 5 minutes before removing from the pan.

Jill Karpisek

Breads & Rolls

Garlic Monkey Bread

1 package dry yeast
1 cup warm (105° to 115°) water
1 teaspoon salt
2 1/2 to 3 cups flour
1 teaspoon sugar

Dip

1/4 cup melted butter or margarine
1 large or 2 small cloves garlic, minced
1/4 teaspoon salt
1 Tablespoon dried parsley flakes

In a large bowl, dissolve yeast in warm water; add sugar and salt. Set aside until bubbly, about 5 minutes. Slowly stir in flour until a soft batter is formed. Beat until smooth. Add more flour to make a stiff dough. It will be too stiff to stir with a spoon. Form into a ball with hands; cover and let rest for 15 minutes. Turn onto a floured surface and knead for 5 minutes. Put into a greased bowl, cover, and let rise until double. Butter a 1 1/2- to 2-quart ring mold.

Mix butter, garlic, and parsley. Divide dough into quarters and then each quarter into pieces the size of a walnut. Dip each piece in the butter mixture and place in the ring mold. Cover and let rise until doubled. Bake at 375° for 25 to 30 minutes.

Fina Smith Distefano

Breads & Rolls

A family favorite.

Lithuanian Bacon Buns

2 pounds bacon, diced
1 medium onion, diced
1 egg
**Bread dough (frozen or your own) for 24 dinner rolls or 1 loaf of
  bread**

Fry bacon until it is brown, but not crispy. Add onion and cook until it is translucent. Drain off fat drippings and save. Cool bacon and onion; stir in egg. Cut dough into 2-inch pieces and roll flat, about 1/2-inch thick. Shape into squares or rectangles. Put about 2 tablespoons of bacon mixture in the middle and fold dough over. Place 2 inches apart on a greased baking sheet. Allow to rise according to dough directions. Bake at 400° for about 20 to 30 minutes until golden brown. Brush tops with reserved drippings, if desired. Cool on paper bags to absorb grease.

Mary Duda

Mr. Bill Orr, husband of former Governor Kay Orr, is the only First Gentleman to date.

Breads & Rolls

Coffee Cake

3/4 cup sugar
1/4 cup soft shortening
1 egg
1 1/2 cups flour
1/2 teaspoon salt
2 teaspoons baking powder
1/2 cup milk

Filling

1/2 cup brown sugar
1 1/2 teaspoons cinnamon

Cream the butter and sugar until light and fluffy. Add the egg. Sift the dry ingredients together. Add to the creamed mixture, alternating with the milk. For the filling mixture, stir together brown sugar and cinnamon. You may either sprinkle all of this mixture on top of the batter or place half of the batter in the pan, half of the filling mixture over the batter, then add the rest of the batter and finally the rest of the filling mixture on top. Grease and flour a 9×9-inch pan. Bake at 375° for 25 to 35 minutes. Let the cake cool briefly before serving.

Maxine Throckmorton-Gestrine, grandmother of Senator Greg Adams

---

While growing up, I spent a lot of time with my Grandmother Maxine, either on the farm west of Osceola, in Osceola, or later at her home in Stromsburg. She made the best homemade bread, and no one will ever top her banana cream pie. I also remember that whenever I visited, Grandma would make this wonderful coffee cake in the morning. I hope you enjoy it.

Senator Greg Adams

A similar recipe was submitted by Erica Fish, daughter of Senator Mark Christensen.

For more years than I can remember, I have made this bread to put in my holiday baskets and given it to friends and family. I have made this with red spiced gumdrops for Valentine's Day, green gumdrops for St. Patrick's Day, and multicolored spiced gumdrops for Christmas. Great either as one loaf or mini loaves, depending on your needs.

SAL's Gumdrop Bread

3 cups sifted all-purpose flour
3/4 cup sugar
3 1/2 teaspoons baking powder
1 teaspoon salt
1 beaten egg
1 1/2 cups milk
2 Tablespoons cooking oil
3/4 cup spiced gumdrops, snipped

Sift together flour, sugar, baking powder, and salt. Combine egg, milk, cooking oil, and gumdrops. Add all at once to dry ingredients, mixing just until combined. Pour into greased and floured 9 × 5 × 3-inch pan or greased and floured mini pans. Bake in 350° oven for 1 hour or until done (a toothpick placed in the middle of the loaf comes out clean). Remove from pan; cool on rack.

SharonAnn Louden

Mom Nelson's Banana Bread

1 1/2 cups sugar
1/2 cup butter
2 eggs
3 to 4 mashed ripe bananas
2 cups flour
1 teaspoon soda
1/4 teaspoon salt
1 teaspoon vanilla
Walnuts to liking (I use 1 to 2 cups, but Mom never did. She would say, "Oh, that is too many!")

Cream butter and sugar together until color lightens and mixture is fluffy. Add eggs gradually, mixing well. Sift dry ingredients and add alternately with mashed bananas to the fat mixture. Add vanilla last. Pour into a greased bread pan. Bake at 350° for 45 to 60 minutes.

Cindy Nelson

This is one of the few, if not the only, written recipe that I have from my mother-in-law, Grace Nelson, Holdrege, Nebraska. From her we got all of our Swedish heritage cooking. Try as we might, we could never get her recipes for such things as rye bread, rice pudding, dopp i grytan, ostkaka, pepparkakor, or lutfisk down on paper. Her answer was always, "Oh, you just take some flour, some sugar, a little of this spice, a little of that spice, some butter, some salt" and whatever else, depending on the dish. The grandkids would even threaten to videotape her while she was actually making the recipe, but she would have none of that. This recipe has always received great raves.

Who does not love the smell of home-baked zucchini bread in the fall? I remember stopping at the roadside stands around Elkhorn to buy zucchini to make this treat.

A similar recipe was supplied by Senator Daniell Nantkes: "This recipe is from Grandma Nantkes and is to be used in late summer when you have extra zucchini from the garden."

Zucchini Bread

2 cups grated, unpeeled zucchini
1 cup raisins
3 cups flour
1 teaspoon salt
1 teaspoon soda
3/4 teaspoon baking powder
1 Tablespoon cinnamon
4 eggs
1 cup vegetable oil
2 cups sugar
1 teaspoon grated lemon peel
1 cup chopped walnuts (optional)

Prepare zucchini and set aside. Rinse raisins and drain. Sift together dry ingredients. Beat eggs well using a mixer. Gradually add sugar, oil, and lemon rinds. Toss raisins with a generous Tablespoon of the dry mixture. Blend in dry ingredients, alternating with grated zucchini into egg mixture. When blended, stir in raisins and nuts. Divide batter into 2 greased and floured loaf pans. Bake at 350° for 55 minutes.

Senator Dwite Pederson

Breads & Rolls

Triple Berry Muffins

2 1/2 teaspoons baking powder
1 egg
1 cup milk
1/2 cup sugar
2 cups flour
3/4 teaspoon sea salt
1/3 cup corn oil
1 teaspoon pure vanilla
1 cup fresh or frozen mixed berries, (blue, black, and raspberries—
    frozen bag of berries from Schwan Food Company works well)

Stir dry ingredients into a bowl. Combine egg, milk, vanilla, and oil. Add all at once to the dry ingredients. Stir quickly just until the dry ingredients are blended. Gently stir in the berries. Fill muffin cups 2/3 full of batter. Sprinkle on muffin topping (recipe below) and bake at 400° for 18 to 25 minutes, just until a light golden brown. Do not overbake. Best if cooled 20 minutes before eating. Leftovers can be frozen and eaten later.

Muffin Topping

2/3 cup brown sugar
1/3 cup flour
2 Tablespoons melted butter

Mix with a fork until a crumbly mixture is formed. Topping can be saved and refrigerated for the next batch of muffins.

Senator Mick and Katie Mines

This recipe is one of my favorites that my kids and their friends have eaten many times. Great with breakfast, as an after-school snack, or for coffee with a friend. You can make the blueberries alone. Sometimes I will add extra berries on top of each muffin just before sprinkling on the topping.

Breads & Rolls

Muffins are a favorite at the Foley home, and these blueberry muffins are at the top of the list.

Oat Bran Blueberry Muffins

Dry ingredients:

**1 cup oat bran
1 1/4 cups all-purpose flour
1/2 cup sugar
3 teaspoons baking powder
3/4 teaspoon salt
1 teaspoon nonfat dry milk**

Wet ingredients:

**3/4 cup milk
1 teaspoon vanilla
2 egg whites
1/4 cup canola oil
1 cup fresh blueberries (or thawed frozen)**

Preheat oven to 375° to 400°. Grease or paper line the muffin pan. In a large bowl, combine all the dry ingredients and mix well. In a medium bowl, combine all the wet ingredients except blueberries and mix well. Combine dry and wet ingredients; stir till just mixed together. Add blueberries and mix briefly. Spoon into muffin pan and bake 20 to 25 minutes. Remove from pan and cool on rack.

Makes 12 muffins.

State Auditor Mike Foley

Breads & Rolls

Apple-Butterscotch Muffins

3 cups flour
1/4 cup sugar
4 teaspoons baking powder
1 1/2 teaspoons salt
2 eggs, beaten
1 1/2 cups milk
1 (6-ounce) package butterscotch chips
1 cup diced Nebraska City apples

Stir together flour, sugar, baking powder, and salt. Combine remaining ingredients in a separate bowl then add all at once to flour mixture. Stir just until flour is moist. Fill greased muffin cups 2/3 full of batter or use paper liners. Bake at 400° to 425° for 20 to 25 minutes or until golden brown.

Kathy Kaufman

Mrs. David Butler was the wife of the first State Governor after Nebraska became a state in 1867.

Six Weeks Raisin Bran Muffins

Treat your family to fresh-baked muffins every morning with this batter that can be kept in the refrigerator for up to six weeks. Many years ago, my dear friend gave me a bowl of this batter. She told me to put it in the refrigerator, and when I wanted one of her muffins, just pop it in the oven or toaster oven.

1 (10-ounce) box Raisin Bran
1 cup shortening (Crisco) melted
3 1/2 cups sugar
4 eggs, beaten
1 quart buttermilk
5 cups flour
5 teaspoons baking soda
2 teaspoons salt

Combine all the ingredients. Fill greased muffin tins or paper cup liners two-thirds full. Bake at 400° for 20 to 25 minutes.

Peggy L. Green

The Governor's Office was one of the first rooms to be remodeled in 1997. An asbestos ceiling was removed, and the fireplace, along with the other three in the house, was converted to gas.

Breads & Rolls

Ingrid's Pepparkaka (Spice Cake)

3 eggs
3/4 cup sugar
2 ounces butter
3/4 cup yogurt (6 ounces coffee or plain)
2 teaspoons cinnamon
2 teaspoons ginger
2 teaspoons cloves
2 teaspoons ground cardamom
1/2 teaspoon salt
1 teaspoon baking soda
1 teaspoon baking powder
1 cup flour

Whip egg and sugar. Melt butter, cool, and blend with yogurt. Combine the dry ingredients. Add the flour mixture in 3 parts, alternating with thirds of the yogurt/butter to the whipped eggs. Stir the batter after each addition until smooth. Set oven at 350°. Bake in a greased and floured pan (1 quart), round or square, for about 30 minutes or until a knife comes out clean from the cake.

Kerstin O'Connor

I remember eating this cake every Christmas Eve morning as we six children sat in the living room, eagerly waiting to open our first Christmas gift. I brought this tradition with me to the States from Sweden.

We use this recipe for our birthday breakfast.

Baking Powder Biscuits

2 cups flour
4 teaspoons baking powder
1/2 teaspoon cream of tartar
1/2 teaspoon salt
2 teaspoons sugar
1/2 cup softened butter or Crisco
1 egg
2/3 cup milk

Mix together the dry ingredients. Cut in the butter or Crisco. Blend egg and milk together and fold into mixture. Do not overstir. Place on floured surface and roll out until 1-inch thick. Cut with biscuit cutter and place on ungreased cookie sheet. Top with sugar and bake at 450° for 12 minutes. Cool on rack. Serve with your favorite topping: honey, butter, strawberries and whipped cream or Cool Whip.

Emilee Fish, daughter of Senator Mark Christensen

Sourdough Biscuit

1 cup unsifted flour
2 Tablespoons sugar
2 teaspoons baking powder
1/2 teaspoon salt
1/2 cup warm milk
1 cup Sourdough Starter (see This and That, page 306)

Place dry ingredients in a bowl. Add the milk and the starter. Mix well and turn out onto a floured board. Knead 8 to 10 times. The dough should be spongy and slightly sticky. Roll out to 1-inch thick dough. Cut out biscuits with a biscuit cutter. Place in a greased pan. (As the biscuits are being placed, turn them over so that the top is greased). Set pan in a warm spot 20 to 30 minutes. Bake in 400° oven about 25 minutes.

LeeAnn Merrihew

There is a story about a secret tunnel leading to the Capitol from a door in the paneling of the Governor's Office. In the 1980s, the door was pried open to reveal only a closet.

Connie's 'Red Lobster' Cheese Garlic Biscuits

2 cups Bisquick
2/3 cups milk
1/2 cup grated cheddar cheese
1/2 cup melted butter
1/4 teaspoon garlic salt

Mix Bisquick, milk, and cheddar cheese until a soft ball forms. Beat vigorously for 30 seconds. Drop by balls onto an ungreased baking sheet and bake at 450° for 8 minutes. Mix butter and garlic, and brush on rolls while still on the pan and hot.

Connie Rothermund

The porch adjoining the Governor's Office was also remodeled in 1997 and enclosed so that it could be used year-round. The design of the Nebraska State Quarter was etched into the glass doors (see photos on page 2).

Corn Bread Jenn

3/4 cup cornmeal
1 cup all-purpose flour
2 to 3 Tablespoons sugar
2 1/2 teaspoons baking powder
3/4 teaspoon salt
1 Tablespoon butter
2 beaten eggs
1 cup of buttermilk or 1 cup half-and-half
1/4 cup cooking oil or melted butter

Optional add-ins:

1/2 to 1 cup fresh or frozen corn, black beans, red beans, or 1/2 cup
   crumbled blue cheese
1 cup shredded cheese for topping

Preheat oven to 400°. Stir together cornmeal, flour, sugar, baking powder, and salt; set aside. Add Tablespoon of butter to a cast-iron skillet or 9-inch round pan; place in 400° oven for 3 minutes or until butter is melted. Swirl around to coat sides and bottom. In a bowl, combine eggs, buttermilk, and oil, and add dry ingredients all at once.

Add additional ingredients, if using, and pour into hot skillet. Bake 15 to 20 minutes until done. After 10 minutes of baking, add shredded cheese on top, if using.

Serves 6 to 8.

Jennifer Beebe

Jennifer's great-great-great-grandfather, the Honorable Henry P. Beebe, was the first member of the Nebraska State Legislature from Dodge County. Her ancestors were among the first arrivals in Dodge County in May 1856. Jenn is a caterer in Lincoln, Nebraska.

This recipe for sourdough buckwheat flapjacks can be mixed up and allowed to stand overnight, all ready for an early breakfast.

Easy Buckwheat Flapjacks

1 cup warm milk
1 cup Sourdough Starter (see This and That, page 306)
1 large egg
1 Tablespoon melted shortening
1 cup buckwheat pancake mix

Combine the 4 first ingredients. Add the pancake mix. Beat well. Cover and set in a cool place. Cook on a hot skillet and serve with Nebraska honey or syrup.

LeeAnn Merrihew

The State Dining Room's walls are covered with a Zuber mural from Paris, Scenic America. The mural was designed in 1834 and handpainted with 1,690 wooden blocks in 233 different colors.

Breads & Rolls

Joel's Cornmeal Pancakes

1 cup buttermilk
1 egg (room temperature)
3 Tablespoons melted butter
1/2 cup all-purpose flour
1/4 cup yellow corn meal
1/2 teaspoon salt
1 teaspoon baking soda
Splash of vanilla

Stir flour, salt, and soda in a bowl. Blend together buttermilk, egg, and melted butter. Stir in dry ingredients to liquid. Mix until smooth. Add vanilla. Let stand for 30 minutes before grilling. Grill on medium, 350°, until golden brown.

Serves 2 to 3.

Senator Joel T. Johnson

Kids say the darndest things! As we were driving in the minivan, my three-year-old son, Bede, noticed a tow truck out his window. "Mom," he asked, "Do tow trucks carry toes?"

Bede's Favorite Pancakes

1 cup flour (white, wheat, soy, or some of each)
3 eggs
1 cup cottage cheese
1/2 cup milk or juice
1/4 cup pumpkin canned—or cooked fresh
1 Tablespoon oil

Blend all ingredients in a blender on high for 2 minutes. Heat skillet to medium-high then add 1 teaspoon oil. After oil has heated to medium heat, add 1/4 cup batter. Cook until bubbles form around the edges. Flip over and cook for another minute. Serve with butter and syrup or applesauce and yogurt.

Senator Tony and Judy Fulton

Ultimate Pancakes and Waffles

2 cups Bisquick mix
1/2 cup oil
1 egg
1 1/3 cups club soda

Mix all ingredients and stir until batter is smooth. Pour in a waffle iron or 1/4 cupfuls onto a hot griddle. Cook until the edges are dry or waffle iron light goes on.

Sam Haberman, grandson of the late Senator Haberman

Breads & Rolls

Aebelskiver

2 cups flour
2 Tablespoons sugar
1 teaspoon baking powder
1 teaspoon baking soda
1/2 teaspoon salt
3 large eggs, separated
2 cups buttermilk
3 Tablespoons butter, melted

Optional:

1/2 teaspoon cardamon
1/2 cup raisins

Mix dry ingredients, including optional cardamom. Beat egg yolks and add to buttermilk. Add dry ingredients and mix. Add melted butter. Add raisins that have been soaked in hot water for a few minutes. Fold in thoroughly beaten egg whites. Bake in aebelskiver pan (a traditional Danish pancake pan) generously greased with shortening over medium heat. Turn baked portion (traditional tool is a knitting needle) in order to bake other half. Serve hot with butter, sugar, applesauce, syrup, or jam.

Professor Norman Bansen

The aebelskiver (Danish pancakes) recipe is from the late Professor Emeritus of English and Dane Norman Bansen, also a 1947 graduate of Dana College. Professor Bansen was known to serve these when he entertained his classes at his home and for friends at weekend brunch. They are still served each year during Homecoming festivities at Dana College, as well as during fundraising breakfasts by Blair Rotary Club and Arlington Lions Club.

This recipe has been handed down over generations. My great-grandmother died the year I was born, 1935. She moved from New York State with husband and children and homesteaded in the Merriman, Nebraska, area. There they made their home with four daughters and one son, until moving to Gordon where she opened a millinery shop. At one point, they moved to Minnesota but soon returned to Nebraska and family. I am sure she fried these "doughy things" in pure lard, the pioneer shortening. With our LDL-and HDL-conscious awareness, we would find that to be a no-no. Anyway, they are delicious.

Grandma Cody's Doughnuts

One cup sugar, one cup milk
Two eggs beaten, fine as silk
Salt, nutmeg, lemon will do
Baking powder—teaspoons two
Lightly stir the flour in
Roll on pie board, not too thin
Cut in diamonds, twists, or rings
Drop with care these doughy things
To fat that briskly swells
Evenly the spongy cells
Watch with care the time for burning
Roll in sugar, serve hot or cold
Warm them in the oven when they get old

Gwen Johnson Otte, Regent, Lone Willow Chapter, DAR, granddaughter of Helen Cady Johnson Spill

German Zwieback

2 cups milk
1 cup butter
1 1/2 cups sugar
1 1/2 cups potato water
2 teaspoons salt
2 packages yeast
4 eggs, beaten
6 to 7 cups flour

Scald 2 cups milk; pour into a large bowl. Add butter, sugar, and salt. When lukewarm, add yeast, the well-beaten eggs, and some flour. Beat hard; let rise until light. Then work in more flour until a soft dough is formed. When light again, cut the dough in pieces about the size of small loaves. Place in well-greased pan and cover; let rise till very light. Bake 25 to 30 minutes in 300° oven. When cold, cut into slices and brown and dry slowly in 350° oven, turning once. Can be sprinkled with butter, sugar, and cinnamon before browning and drying.

Marlene Bunger Sanders

This recipe originated in the late 1800s.

Mom's Knäckebröd (Swedish Hardtack)

2 cups Total Cereal, crush after measuring
2 cups white flour, plus additional when rolling
2 cups quick-cooking oatmeal
1 cup margarine
1/3 cup sugar
1/2 teaspoon salt
1 cup warm water
1 teaspoon baking soda

Mix dry ingredients with margarine, like for pie crust. Add water mixed with baking soda. Mix well. Chill for several hours. Roll thin, using additional flour as necessary. Make indentions with special rolling pin or prick with a fork. Bake irregular pieces on cookie sheets at 325° for 5 to 6 minutes (maybe longer). Complete the drying on pastry rack. Place in oven that has been heated and turned off. Leave overnight to ensure crispness.

Mary Anderson

The Blue Danube china and Meissen candlesticks from the first Residence are displayed in the Family Dining Room.

Ashland, Nebraska, artist Judy Graff painted the artwork in the Family Dining Room entitled *9 to 5*

Breads & Rolls

The original Family Dining Room.

Soups, Salads & Vegetables

The Family Dining Room

The Family Dining Room has been a favorite of First Families who have lived in the Residence. This room houses the Blue Danube china and candlesticks that were used in the original mansion. The Family Dining Room provides the perfect spot for private meetings and meals.

The Sun Porch provides a relaxing setting for the First Family to enjoy the seasons of Nebraska while sheltered from the elements.

The Sun Porch is a wonderful environment for plants, as evidenced by the blooming Christmas cactus that has been part of the Residence for many years.

Soups, Salads & Vegetables

Jim's Chili

2 pounds ground beef
1 pound pork sausage
1 whole onion
1 quart tomato juice
1 (8-ounce) can tomato sauce
1 (12- to 15-ounce) can whole peeled tomatoes
2 cans red or kidney beans
1 large green pepper, diced
1 Tablespoon vinegar
1 clove garlic, peeled
Dash of cayenne pepper
Dash of regular black pepper
2 Tablespoons chili powder
1 to 2 dehydrated jalapeño peppers (may use bottled or canned ones)

Brown beef, pork, and chopped onion in a skillet. Drain off grease. Add meat mixture and the rest of the ingredients to a kettle and cook for 1 hour. Pork may be omitted and recipe can be cut in half.

Makes 4 quarts.

Former First Lady Ruth Thone

*Our family **loves** soup, and I make it throughout the year. In the winter, I make chili, all kinds of vegetable soups, and chicken soup. During the summer, I make cold soups, such as gazpacho, cucumber, and zucchini. But this is our very favorite vegetable soup and has been in my recipe file for close to thirty years. Our children crave it, and I always make a double batch so there is plenty leftover for them to take some home with them. It is delicious, filling, and is so easy to make. The best part about it is that it is made in the Crock-Pot, so it is easy for busy families to eat it whenever they are ready. With four children in our family, it was perfect to have ready when they all came home from their after-school activities.*

Easy Gourmet Vegetable Beef Soup

2 pounds stew meat cut into 1-inch cubes
2 Tablespoons margarine
2 medium russet potatoes cut into 1-inch cubes
1 onion, chopped
2 cups chopped celery
4 carrots, pared and sliced
1/2 of a small head cabbage, chopped
1 can (46-ounce) V8 Juice
1 Tablespoon salt
1 teaspoon seasoned pepper

Brown meat on all sides in margarine in a large, heavy pan. Add meat and remaining ingredients to a large Crock-Pot and cook on low for 10 hours. If too thick, add water.

Makes 3 quarts.

Former First Lady Diane Nelson

Soups, Salads & Vegetables

German Noodles and Butterballs Soup

Yellow egg noodles
5 eggs
1 2/3 cups flour

Mix the eggs, then add the flour and mix well. Roll flat to thinner than pie dough. Roll up like newspaper and slice on cutting board into long noodle strands. Fluff and separate noodles. Dry them and store for future use.

Butter Balls

4 cups white dry bread crumbs
1/2 cup melted oleo or butter
4 eggs
1/4 cup sweet cream, warmed
1 cup browned bread crumbs, toasted and sifted
1/4 teaspoon salt
1/2 teaspoon allspice

Put crumbs in large bowl. Pour butter over crumbs. Add beaten eggs and salt. Pour warm cream over mixture. Using hands, mix thoroughly until mixture can be formed in walnut-sized balls. If balls fall apart, add another egg. Then drop balls into boiling water. When ball comes to surface, it is done (just a few minutes).

To combine for soup, cook butter balls in chicken broth and then add noodles.

Margaret Erdman, Senator Philip and Cortney Erdman's grandmother

This is a very special meal for the Erdman family. It is a German dish and a family favorite. At every special meal, it is served.

This Scandinavian recipe has become a Christmas season favorite for our family. It is delicious any time of day and may be kept warm in a Crock-Pot. Refrigerated, it lasts for days!

Fruit Soup

3/4 cup dried apricots, quartered
3/4 cup prunes, quartered
3/4 cup raisins (white)
7 cups water
1/2 cup sugar
1 to 2 cinnamon sticks
3 to 4 Tablespoons tapioca
1/2 cup currant jelly
1/4 cup orange juice
2 Tablespoons lemon juice
1/2 cup fresh cooking apple, sliced and peeled
1 cup sweet bing cherries, drained and halved

A 4-quart kettle is large enough for this size batch. Soak apricots, raisins, and prunes in water (7 cups) overnight or at least 8 hours (covered). Add sugar and cinnamon and cook over medium heat. When contents are warm, add tapioca. Then cook covered for 30 minutes, stirring frequently. Add juices and all other fruit. Cook uncovered for 5 minutes or until clear and slightly thickened. Continue to stir. Serve hot or cold. Garnish with orange and lemon slices.

Senator John and Judy Nelson

Spicy Potato Soup

1 pound ground beef
4 cups cubed peeled potatoes (1/2-inch cubes)
1 small onion, chopped
3 (8-ounce) cans tomato sauce
4 cups water
2 teaspoons pepper
1/2 to 1 teaspoon hot pepper sauce

In a Dutch oven or large kettle, brown ground beef. Drain. Add potatoes, onion, and tomato sauce. Stir in water, salt, pepper, and hot pepper sauce. Bring to a boil. Reduce heat and simmer for 1 hour or until the potatoes are tender and the soup has thickened.

Makes 6 to 8 servings.

Lieutenant Governor Rick Sheehy

This recipe is very easy and has a bit of a bite to it. Great for game days.

Soups, Salads & Vegetables

Formed in the heart of Legislative District #4, Boys Town has been recognized and praised both nationally and internationally for its mission of helping young people. Hollywood paid homage to its founder, Father Flanagan, and its mission in the 1938 MGM movie Boys Town, *starring Spencer Tracy, Maureen O'Sullivan, and Mickey Rooney. Over 30,000 Omahans turned out to greet the stars as they arrived to watch the movie premiere in Omaha. In honor of this acclaimed institution, this recipe is submitted. Rest assured, "It ain't heavy, it's my butternut soup..."*

Boys Town Butternut Squash and Apple Soup

2 Tablespoons unsalted butter
1 1/2 cups sliced leeks, white parts only
1 Tablespoon minced garlic
6 cups peeled and roughly diced butternut squash
3 cups peeled and roughly diced apples
2 teaspoons Toasted Spice Rub (recipe follows)
6 1/2 cups chicken stock or 2 (14 1/2-ounce) cans low-sodium chicken broth mixed with 3 cups water
Sea salt, preferably gray salt
1 cup chopped, spiced candied walnuts (optional)

Melt butter in a large pot over medium heat and cook until it turns nut brown. Add the leeks and cook until slightly softened, about 2 minutes. Add the garlic and sauté briefly to release its fragrance. Add the squash and apples. Raise the heat to high and cook, stirring until the vegetables begin to caramelize, about 5 minutes. Stir in the Toasted Spice Rub (below) and cook briefly to toast it, about 1 minute. Add the stock or broth-water mixture, bring to a simmer, and partially cover. Adjust the heat to maintain a gentle simmer and cook until the squash and apples are tender, about 40 minutes. Transfer in batches to a blender or food processor and blend until smooth. Return to the pot, reheat to serving temperature, and season with salt. Divide the soup among warmed bowls and garnish each portion with some of the walnuts, if using. Serve immediately.

Toasted Spice Rub

1/4 cup fennel seeds
1 Tablespoon coriander seeds
1 Tablespoon black peppercorns

Soups, Salads & Vegetables

1 1/2 teaspoons crushed red pepper flakes
1/4 cup chili powder (about 1 ounce)
2 Tablespoons kosher salt
2 Tablespoons ground cinnamon

In a small, heavy pan over medium heat, combine the seeds and peppercorns. When the fennel turns light brown, work quickly. Turn on the exhaust fan; add the red pepper flakes, and toss, toss, toss, always under the fan. Immediately turn the spice mixture out onto a plate to cool. Put in a blender with the chili powder, salt, and cinnamon and blend until the spices are evenly ground. If you have a small spice mill/coffee grinder dedicated to grinding spices, grind only the fennel, coriander, pepper, and chili flakes. Pour into a bowl and toss with the remaining ingredients.

Senator Pete and Lori Pirsch

The lower level conference room is used as a gallery for Nebraska artists. A commission chooses a different artist each month and invites them to display their work.

Soups, Salads & Vegetables

Homemade Tomato Soup

4 medium tomatoes
1 teaspoon basil
1 stick butter
1 teaspoon soda
4 cups regular milk
Pepper, to taste

Peel and cut tomatoes into quarters. Remove seeds if you wish. Sauté tomatoes in butter with basil until hot. Shut off heat and add soda. Cool and add milk. To reheat, use low heat.

Evelyn Robertson

The chandeliers in the State Dining Room are hand-cut Czechoslovakian crystal. The smaller two were originally in the drawing room. Once, when the center chandelier was being cleaned, it was twisted around until it fell and broke. A replacement was ordered but when it arrived, it too had some broken pieces. There were enough pieces from both to reassemble the chandelier, except for one piece that does not match. Even though the chandeliers were cleaned and restrung during restoration, this little piece of history was not replaced.

Soups, Salads & Vegetables

Chili Soup

2 pounds hamburger
Salt
1 white onion, chopped
1 (15-ounce) can whole tomatoes
2 ribs celery
2 large carrots
Jalapeño (optional)
3 teaspoons cumin powder
1 teaspoon onion powder
4 Tablespoons chili powder
2 teaspoons dried chili flakes
1/2 teaspoon paprika
Salt and pepper to taste
1/2 can of beef broth
1 (15-ounce) can tomato sauce
1 can kidney beans, drained and rinsed (can add more to your liking)
1 can red beans, drained and rinsed (add more beef broth if too thick)

Brown hamburger, then add onion and cook until tender. Transfer meat and onion into baking dish—I use my ceramic clay baking dish for this. Puree the vegetable, because most people don't like veggies in their chili, but this adds great flavor and the carrots add that gentle touch of sweetness you need. Don't puree if you like your chili chunky. Add the spices to the meat mixture. Bake covered 1 1/2 hours at 350°. This makes the meat very tender and flavorful. Make your chili spicier by adding more chili or peppers if you like. Next add the tomato sauce and beans. Bake 1 more hour.

Senator Mick and Katie Mines

This is my first-place, award-winning chili recipe! The 2006 Chili Queen! Our church has an annual chili cook-off for a mission's fundraiser each winter. This is the first time I had entered, and to my surprise I won first place.

It is best, after the second baking, to cool and refrigerate overnight, reheat the second day, and then eat. The flavors have time to meld together—it is worth the wait!

Soups, Salads & Vegetables

A recipe from my friend Norma that my children absolutely love!

Norma's White Chili

1 1/2 pounds chicken breast or tenders, shredded
3 cans great northern white beans
1 (10-ounce) can Ro-Tel tomatoes
1 onion, chopped
1 Tablespoon vegetable oil
2 cloves garlic, minced
1 small can chopped green chilies
1 1/2 teaspoons ground cumin
2 teaspoons oregano
1/4 to 1 teaspoon cayenne pepper
  (depending on how spicy you want it)
Salt and pepper, to taste
1 (14-ounce) can chicken broth or use stock from chicken
1 small container sour cream
1 cup shredded Monterey Jack cheese

Cook chicken in boiling water until tender. Place beans (including liquid) and tomatoes in a Crock-Pot set on high, or large pot if cooking on stove.

While chicken is cooking, sauté onions in a skillet with oil. Add garlic and chilies and cook until onions are tender. Add seasonings and cook 2 minutes. Add to bean mixture. Add broth and shredded chicken and cook for 1 hour in the Crock-Pot or 30 minutes if in large pot on stove. Stir in sour cream until melted. Add shredded cheese a little at a time, stirring until melted. Enjoy!

Toni Blazevich

Soups, Salads & Vegetables

Halibut Chowder

1 cup onions, chopped
2 cups celery, chopped
2 Tablespoons oil
4 cups potatoes, chopped
1 teaspoon salt
1 teaspoon pepper
8 cups water
2 cups chicken stock
2 cups cream
4 cups fresh halibut, chopped
Chopped parsley

Sauté the onions and celery in the oil. Add the potatoes, salt, and pepper. Cover with water and boil until tender. Add chicken stock and bring to a boil. Reduce to a simmer and stir in the cream.

Add the halibut and bring back just to a simmer. (Don't overcook or the chowder will taste fishy and the cream may curdle.) Ladle in bowls, garnishing with chopped parsley.

Serves 8 to 10.

Wes Sheets

On the first day out of port on a six-day fishing excursion around southeastern Alaska, I had hooked an expensive bait 300 feet deep on a submerged mountaintop, or so I thought. After handing my friend, the guide, the pole to retrieve the hook, he tugged on it a couple of times. Handing it back, he said to just reel it in. Well, I tried, and it seemed to still be hooked on the bottom until all of the sudden the bottom decided to move. The fight was on for over an hour just to land that dandy halibut. I believe I learned how good it is when we cooked that fish with this chowder recipe.

Soups, Salads & Vegetables

Seafood Chowder

2 cups celery, chopped
2 cups onion, chopped
6 medium potatoes, cubed
1/2 cup carrots, chopped
2 (6 1/2-ounce) cans minced clams
1 (6 1/2-ounce) cans minced crab
1 (4 1/2-ounce) can tiny shrimp
2 Tablespoons Worcestershire sauce
Salt
Pepper
2 sticks oleo or butter
6 Tablespoons flour
6 cups milk or cream

Cook together celery, onions, potatoes, and carrots until done. Save the water for soup. Add clams, crab meat, shrimp, Worcestershire sauce, salt, and pepper to taste. In large pan, melt butter, then add flour to make paste and gradually add milk or cream to make white sauce. Add the first mixture and let come to a boil but do not boil. More milk or cream can be added if you want a thinner soup.

Serves 8 to 10.

Wes Sheets

Hearty Beef and Sausage Stew

1 Tablespoon salad oil
1 pound stewing beef, cut in 1/2-inch cubes
1 pound sweet Italian sausage, sliced (or sausage of your choice)
1 cup onion, chopped
1 teaspoon salt
1 (28-ounce) can chopped tomatoes
2 1/2 cups water
1 Tablespoon Worcestershire sauce
1 cup sliced celery
2 cups potatoes, cut in 1/2-inch cubes

In a large soup pot, heat oil until hot. Add beef, brown on all sides, remove with slotted spoon and set aside. Add sausage and brown. Drain off drippings. Add tomatoes, water, onions, salt, Worcestershire, and beef. Bring to a boil, then reduce heat. Simmer covered until beef is almost tender, about 1 1/2 hours. Add potatoes and celery. Simmer covered until vegetables and meat are tender, 30 to 45 minutes.

Cynthia and Norman Monroe

We were in Minneapolis to visit my cousin for a few days and the right distance for a motorcycle trip from Lincoln. However, when we arrived in Minneapolis, it was very chilly and very rainy, and we were very cold. We took a wrong turn and became lost in the city, and took an extra hour of being very cold looking for my cousin's home. Once we found it, we went inside, took off our wet clothes, and enjoyed the wonderful smell of dinner on the stove. This wonderful beef-and-sausage stew, which eventually became our favorite, was hearty and hot, and warmed us as if we were in front of a fireplace with a comforter. This is now a traditional part of our Christmas Eve family soup supper.

I obtained this recipe while I was a Visiting Professor of Political Science at Warsaw University, Poland, during 1980–81. It was ancient custom for Polish hunters to put a pot of stew on an open fire at the start of their hunting day. As the hunt progressed, hunters would return to the fire and add various meats to the pot. By the end of the day, the stew had simmered for several hours, blending the rich flavors of sour cabbage, wild boar, and various other items, making for a hearty meal at the end of the hunt.

Bigos (Traditional Hunter's Stew)

2 pounds sauerkraut
2 pounds white cabbage
1 large white onion, chopped
8 slices bacon
3 pounds meats (ham, Polish sausage, beef, best to have about 3/4 pork)
2 bay leaves
8 mushrooms, cut into quarters
10 peppercorns, whole
2 cups dry red wine

Fry bacon and drain, add onion, and sauté until onion is soft. Drain part of liquid from sauerkraut and add sauerkraut, bacon, and onion to a large pot. Add 1 bay leaf and all the peppercorns. Simmer for 1 hour. Add cabbage, salt, and pepper to taste. Add 1 cup of wine. Simmer another hour. Add all the meats, mushrooms, remaining bay leaf, and cup of wine. Simmer 1 more hour. Note: Always simmer on low heat. This dish gets better with long simmering and reheating. Makes great leftovers.

Senator Bill and Ann Avery

Soups, Salads & Vegetables

Mulligan Stew

2 pounds stew meat
4 cups tomato juice
1/2 cup onion, chopped
4 Tablespoons minute tapioca
2 cups chopped celery
2 Tablespoons sugar
2 cups chopped carrots
8 potatoes, cut into fourths

Mix all ingredients together. Put in roaster or slow cooker. Salt and pepper to taste. Cook with lid on for 5 hours in 250° oven.

Senator Cap and Gloria Dierks

What better way to spend St. Patrick's Day than in O'Neill, Nebraska! There is the crowning of the King and Queen and a parade that VIPs wouldn't dare miss being a part of, especially in an election year. There have been sightings of a green horse more than once. The lovely colleens known as the Irish Dancers perform on the giant shamrock in the square at noon on this holiday. For many years now, spirits and tummies are warmed at St. Patrick's parish hall with this delicious treat ... Mulligan Stew.

An Irish blessing: May the road rise up to meet you. May the wind be always at your back. May the sun shine warm upon your face and the rain fall soft upon your fields. And, until we meet again, may God hold you in the palm of his hand.

Soups, Salads & Vegetables

This fruit salad is a favorite at the Foley home. It is quick and easy and has a wonderful flavor.

Nebraska-Style Fruit Salad

Small box of vanilla instant pudding mix
1 (20-ounce) can of pineapple tidbits, reserve juice
1 (30-ounce) can of fruit cocktail
2 apples, sliced into small pieces
2 to 3 bananas, sliced
Any additional fruit of your choice

Drain the juice from the pineapples and mix the juice with the pudding. Add the sliced apple pieces and mix well so that the vanilla mixture coats the apples. Add the pineapple tidbits. Drain the fruit cocktail and dump the fruit into the vanilla mixture. Add any other fruit. Cover the serving bowl and chill in the fridge. Add sliced bananas just before serving so they don't turn brown.

State Auditor Mike and Susan Foley

Broccoli Slaw

3 stalks celery, sliced
1 bunch green onions, sliced
1 package sliced almonds
1/2 cup shelled sunflower seeds
1 bag prepackaged broccoli slaw
1/3 cup salad oil
1/4 cup sugar

Combine first 5 ingredients in a large bowl. Mix oil and sugar together and pour over the entire mixture.

Attorney General Jon Bruning

When the Legislature passed a bill "to provide a Governor's Mansion, to purchase, pay for and furnish same and to appropriate the sum of $25,000 or as much there-of as needed" in 1899, they neglected to appropriate money for repair and maintenance. Only two years later, both of the first governors to occupy the Residence objected to its neglect, to the point that a bill to sell the Residence passed the Senate but seems to have been dropped in the House (Nebraska's current unicameral system was not instituted until 1937). Instead, the Legislature appropriated $3,000 a year for repair, furnishing, and maintenance of the Residence.

Soups, Salads & Vegetables

This recipe has an unusual list of ingredients, but it's not only tasty, it's also very healthy (224 calories per serving).

Black Bean Shrimp Salad

1 pound cooked medium shrimp, peeled and deveined
1 can (15-ounce) black beans, rinsed and drained
1 small green pepper, julienned
1 small onion, thinly sliced
1/2 cup celery, chopped
2/3 cup picante sauce
2 Tablespoons fresh cilantro, minced
2 Tablespoons lime juice
2 Tablespoons olive oil
2 Tablespoons honey
1/2 teaspoon salt
6 lettuce leaves
1 cup halved cherry tomatoes

In a large bowl, combine the first 5 ingredients. In a small bowl, whisk the picante sauce, cilantro, lime juice, oil, honey, and salt. Pour over shrimp mixture and toss to coat. Cover and refrigerate for at least 2 hours.

Using a slotted spoon, spoon onto a lettuce-lined serving platter or salad plates. Garnish with tomatoes.

Lieutenant Governor Rick Sheehy

Soups, Salads & Vegetables

Festive Tossed Salad

1/2 cup sugar
1/3 cup cider or red wine vinegar
2 Tablespoons lemon juice
2 Tablespoons onion, finely chopped
1/2 teaspoon salt
2/3 cup vegetable oil
2 to 3 teaspoons poppy seed
10 cups torn romaine lettuce
1 cup shredded Swiss cheese
1 medium apple, cored and chopped
1 medium pear, cored and cubed
1/4 cup dried cranberries
1/2 to 1 cup chopped cashews

In a blender or food processor, combine the sugar, vinegar, lemon juice, onion, and salt. Cover and process until blended. With blender running, gradually add oil. Add poppy seeds and blend. In a salad bowl, combine the romaine, cheese, apple, pear, and cranberries. Drizzle with desired amount of dressing. Add cashews; toss to coat. Serve immediately. (There is more than enough dressing if you want to increase the other ingredients a little bit for a larger group.)

Makes 8 to 10 servings.

Senator Dave and Lori Pankonin

Festive Green Salad is a hit no matter what the season. The dried cranberries infuse a spark of red to make one think of Christmas. All of the fresh fruit makes one think spring and summer. It is a year-round pleaser.

My mother copied this recipe from the program Kitchen Klatter *on KMA Radio in Shenandoah, Iowa, in 1940. She always served this to her card club and special company. I use it also for many special occasions. Everyone asks for the recipe.*

Chicken Salad

3 1/2 cups diced chicken
1 cup white seedless grapes
1 1/2 cups pineapple
1/2 cup celery, diced
1/2 cup slivered almonds
3/4 cup mayonnaise
1/2 cup salad dressing
1 teaspoon curry powder

Cut grapes in half and drain pineapple very thoroughly. Combine chicken, grapes, pineapple, celery, and almonds. Set aside. Combine mayonnaise, salad dressing, and curry powder, then stir into chicken mixture. Chill and serve on a lettuce leaf.

Beulah Patton

Soups, Salads & Vegetables

Taffy Apple Salad

1 (15-ounce) can of pineapple chunks
2 cups miniature marshmallows
1 beaten egg
2 Tablespoons flour
1 1/2 teaspoons white vinegar
1/2 cup sugar
2 cups chopped Nebraska City apples
1/2 cup chopped nuts (walnuts or pecans)
1 (8-ounce) container Cool Whip

Prepare this salad 1 day ahead of serving. Drain the pineapple, saving the juice. Mix drained pineapple and marshmallows. Refrigerate overnight. Heat the pineapple juice, egg, flour, vinegar, and sugar. Cook on low heat until thick, stirring well. Refrigerate overnight.

The following day, combine refrigerated ingredients, chopped apples, and nuts. Fold in the Cool Whip and chill until ready to serve. Optional: Can drizzle top of salad with caramel sauce.

Pat Friedli

This was a first-place winner in the Nebraska City/AppleJack Recipe Contest.

Strawberry Nut Salad

2 packages (3-ounce) strawberry gelatin
1 cup hot water
2 packages (10-ounce) frozen strawberries, thawed
1 can (1-pound, 4-ounce) crushed pineapple, drained
3 medium bananas, mashed
1 cup chopped walnuts
1 pint sour cream

Combine gelatin and water. Mix together strawberries (with juice), pineapple, bananas, and nuts. Fold in strawberry mixture to gelatin. Turn half of mixture into 12 × 8 × 2-inch dish. Refrigerate until firm. Spread with sour cream. Gently spoon remaining strawberry mixture over sour cream and then top with remaining sour cream. Refrigerate until firm.

Elva Hansen

Cauliflower and Broccoli Salad

1 head broccoli (use flowers with a little stem cut into bite-size pieces)
1 head cauliflower, cut into bite-size pieces
1 small bottle Wish-Bone Italian Salad Dressing
1/2 onion, chopped
4 fresh mushrooms, sliced
1 can pitted ripe olives, drained
1 cup real mayonnaise
3 to 4 Tablespoons chili sauce
2 teaspoons dill weed
1 teaspoon salt

Marinate broccoli, cauliflower, and onion in salad dressing overnight. Next day, add olives and mushrooms. Stir. Combine mayonnaise, chili sauce, dill weed, and salt. Toss with broccoli mixture and chill for about 2 hours. Will keep for 2 or 3 days.

Amanda Stuthman

This recipe, originally know as Blended Pear Salad, probably came from a magazine advertisement. Its creamy, mild-flavored, fruity gelatin suits all ages. I made it for our family dinners when my grandchildren were very small and soon they began to ask me to fix that "Green Stuff." It's great with turkey, chicken, ham, and roast beef. My grownup granddaughters have launched Green Stuff in their newly married lives on the East and West coasts. However, when they come back to Nebraska, we always have to have Green Stuff at our family celebrations.

Green Stuff

1 (15- to 16-ounce) can pears, drained and reserved
1 (3-ounce) package lime gelatin
1 Tablespoon of lemon juice (if you want it a little more tart)
1 (8-ounce) package cream cheese, slightly softened
1 (8-ounce) container frozen whipped topping
1/2 cup pecans, chopped (optional)
Chopped red maraschino cherries (optional)

Heat the drained pear juice to boiling. Dissolve the gelatin in the hot juice, adding lemon juice if desired. Mash the drained pears and blend in slightly softened cream cheese. (A blender works fine, too.) Slowly blend cooled gelatin and juice into the pear-cheese mixture. Chill until almost set and blend in the unfrozen whipped topping. If you want to add the pecans and cherries, do so at this step. This can become an easy diet salad when you use sugar-free gelatin, fat-free cream cheese, and fat-free whipped topping. This is good for Christmas with the red cherries, but also festive for Easter or any other holiday or birthday.

Clarice A. Orr

Soups, Salads & Vegetables

Tim's Potato Salad

2 pounds baby potatoes, steamed or boiled (with skins on), sliced into 2-inch pieces
2 celery stalks, chopped
1 red onion, chopped
1/4 cup fresh dill, chopped
1/4 cup fresh parsley, chopped

Combine ingredients listed above in a large bowl.

Mix the dressing:

1 cup mayonnaise (fat-free works well, too)
1 teaspoon celery seed
1/4 cup Dijon mustard
1 teaspoon cayenne pepper
1 Tablespoon white wine vinegar
1 to 2 teaspoons lemon juice
Salt and pepper, to taste

Combine the dressing with the potato mixture. Refrigerate.

Tim Earl

I loved this recipe, especially when we had fundraisers in Old Alexandria, Virginia. It was always a big hit. No leftovers!

Walnut Tuna Salad

2 cans tuna, drained and flaked
1 large red apple
1/3 cup celery, chopped
1/3 cup raisins
1/3 cup dates, chopped
1/4 cup walnuts, chopped
1/2 cup fat-free plain yogurt
1/2 cup reduced-fat mayonnaise
4 cups lettuce
1/4 cup shredded Monterey Jack cheese

Combine first 6 ingredients. Mix yogurt and mayo and add to tuna mixture and toss. Sprinkle with cheese.

Congressman Bill and Elsie Barrett

Soups, Salads & Vegetables

BLT Macaroni Salad

2 cups uncooked elbow macaroni
5 green onions, finely chopped
1 large tomato, diced
1 1/4 cups celery, diced
1 1/4 cups mayonnaise
5 teaspoons white vinegar
1/4 teaspoon salt
1/8 teaspoon pepper
1 pound bacon, cooked and crumbled

Cook macaroni according to package directions; drain and rinse in cold water. In a large bowl, combine the macaroni, green onions, tomato, and celery. In a small bowl, combine mayonnaise, vinegar, salt, and pepper. Pour over macaroni mixture and toss to coat. Cover and chill for 2 hours. Just before serving, add bacon.

Pam Johnson

This is a great hot-weather salad, and I also like it with BLT sandwiches.

Soups, Salads & Vegetables

Since 1957, the Louden family ranch branding has begun at 6:30 a.m. on the first Tuesday in June. Senator Louden's mother, Andrea, established the thirteen-item menu that is prepared by our family. The day has grown to now serving about forty family members, neighbors, and friends, some from as far away as Germany, wanting to experience the adventure. Eleven original items continue, with the addition of wild-crafted creamed asparagus in the 1960s and this taco salad in the 1970s.

Andrea's Branding Taco Salad

1 1/2 pounds ground beef
1 medium onion, finely chopped
Salt
Pepper
2 1/2 heads lettuce, finely sliced
1 package finely shredded Colby Jack cheese
1 bag Fritos Original Corn Chips
2 tomatoes, chopped and drained
Sliced black olives (optional)
Sliced jalapeños (optional)

Dressing

1 1/2 cups Dorothy Lynch Salad Dressing
1 1/2 cups mayonnaise
1 1/2 envelopes mild taco seasoning

Mix ingredients for the dressing and set aside. Brown ground beef, onion, salt, and pepper (to taste), breaking beef into small pieces. Drain and cool. In a large bowl, mix in this order: lettuce with ground beef; add tomatoes, cheese, and salad dressing, combining thoroughly. Minutes before serving, add Fritos and mix well. Keep salad cool so chips, lettuce, and cheese remain firm. Enjoy!

Serves approximately 40.

Andrea Louden, 1902–2005
Senator LeRoy and SharonAnn Louden

Soups, Salads & Vegetables

Perfection Salad

1 envelope Knox Unflavored Gelatin
1/4 cup granulated sugar
1/2 teaspoon salt
1 1/4 cups water
1/4 cup vinegar
1 Tablespoon lemon juice
1/2 cup cabbage, shredded
1 pimiento, cut in small pieces or 2 Tablespoons sweet red or green
   bell pepper, chopped

Mix gelatin, sugar, and salt thoroughly in a small saucepan. Add 1/2 cup water. Place over low heat, stirring until gelatin is dissolved. Remove from heat and stir in remaining 3/4 cup of water, vinegar, and lemon juice. Chill mixture to unbeaten egg-white consistency. Fold in cabbage, celery, and pimiento (or pepper). Pour into 8 × 8-inch square dish and chill until firm. Cut into squares and serve with favorite salad dressing.

Wilma L. Lorenz

This recipe is one my maternal grandmother, Anna Stejskal Most Chaney, made for holiday dinners. especially in the hot summers as I was growing up in Aurora, Nebraska. Anna was the seventh child born to Frank and Anna Stastny Stejskal, who came to America from Czechoslovakia via Chicago in 1871 and homesteaded near Wilber in Saline County. Anna was born in 1887 in Saline County and died January 5, 1995, in Grand Island at the age of 107. She always baked on Fridays, so it was a mission to stop on the way home from school to see if there were bismarks, kolaces, rye bread, cinnamon rolls, or angel-food cake for a snack!

Soups, Salads & Vegetables

This recipe comes from Prairie Potpourri and was served after a Legislative League Outing to Bess Streeter Aldrich Museum and Home.

Romaine and Artichoke Salad

Salad

1 (8-ounce) can artichokes, cut into eighths (not marinated)
1 head romaine lettuce
4 Tablespoons fresh green onions, chopped
1/2 cup slivered or sliced almonds, toasted and buttered in oven
   (drain on towel and salt heavily)
Black olives, chopped, quantity to your taste

Dressing

3/4 cup oil
6 Tablespoons red wine vinegar
1/2 cup sugar

Refrigerate artichokes in dressing overnight or for several hours. Toss together with rest of ingredients and serve.

Senator Dave and Lori Pankonin

Soups, Salads & Vegetables

Chinese Chicken Toss

4 cups diced, cooked chicken
2 (1-pound) cans bean sprouts
2 cups cooked rice
2 cups chopped celery
2 cups chopped carrots
4 Tablespoons chopped green pepper
1/2 cup chopped onion
1 1/2 cups mayonnaise
3/4 cup French dressing or Dorothy Lynch Salad Dressing
5 Tablespoons soy sauce
1 teaspoon salt
1 small package slivered almonds
2 cans water chestnuts (optional)

Mix all ingredients and refrigerate until ready to eat. This makes a large salad, so you can cut it in half.

Ruth Newill

Ruth's daughter served this at a restaurant in Oakland, Nebraska, and it was a weekly favorite.

Soups, Salads & Vegetables

This is a favorite family recipe that adults and kids all like. My mother often served this vegetable dish at brandings and large family gatherings.

Creamed Green Beans with Onions

3 Tablespoons butter or margarine
1 teaspoon dry mustard
1/4 teaspoon pepper
1 (1-pound) can or jar small whole onions, drained
12 slices American cheese
2 Tablespoons flour
1 teaspoon salt
1 cup half-and-half
2 (1-pound) cans French-style green beans, drained
1/2 cup chopped nuts

In large saucepan, melt butter. Stir in flour, mustard, salt, and pepper. Cook and stir over low heat until mixture is bubbly. Gradually stir in half-and-half. Stir in vegetables. In 8-inch square baking dish, place one-third vegetable mixture. Top with 4 slices cheese. Repeat 2 times, ending with cheese and then nuts. Bake uncovered for 30 minutes in preheated 350° oven. Can make a day ahead and refrigerate, increasing baking time 10 minutes.

Gladys Jorgenson

Soups, Salads & Vegetables

Eggplant Gratin

Olive oil
3 eggplants, peeled and sliced (salt and pepper each slice)
Salt
Pepper
1 onion, finely chopped
2 cloves garlic, minced
1 pound fresh tomatoes, chopped
1/4 cup ricotta cheese
2 eggs
1/2 cup grated Parmesan cheese
1/2 cup heavy cream

Sauté eggplant in a skillet (with salt, pepper, and olive oil) until golden brown. Sauté onions in olive oil until golden brown and add garlic, then tomatoes, salt, and pepper. Simmer until moisture evaporates. In a mixing bowl, whisk eggs, ricotta cheese with salt, pepper, cream, and half of the grated parmesan cheese.

In medium baking dish, alternate eggplant slices, Parmesan cheese, and tomato mixture. Pour over the baking dish the cheese-egg mixture. Sprinkle remaining Parmesan cheese on top. Bake at 350° until golden brown, about 40 minutes.

Serves 4.

Kelly Sutton

Soups, Salads & Vegetables

Potatoes Florentine

6 medium potatoes, peeled and quartered
2 teaspoons salt
1/4 teaspoon white pepper
2 Tablespoons milk
1 cup sour cream
1/2 cup butter
2 teaspoons dried chives
1 teaspoon dill weed
**1 (10-ounce) package frozen chopped spinach, thawed and squeeze
   dried**
1 cup grated cheddar cheese

Cook, drain, and mash potatoes. Add salt, pepper, milk, sour cream, and butter; beat until smooth. Stir in chives, dill weed, and spinach. Place in buttered casserole. Top with cheese and bake at 400° for 30 minutes.

Kristi Leckband

Harvest Squash

2 acorn squash, about 1 pound each
2 large tart apples, pared and thinly sliced
1/2 cup slivered almonds
1/2 cup raisins or dried cranberries
1 1/2 teaspoons apple pie spice
1 cup maple syrup
1 Tablespoon lemon juice
1/4 cup butter
1/4 cup cornstarch
1/4 teaspoon salt

Halve squash, remove seeds. Place cut side down in a shallow greased pan. Bake at 350° for 30 minutes. Turn squash right side up. Combine apples, almonds, and raisins. Fill squash centers with this mixture. Combine remaining ingredients in a small saucepan, cook and stir until thickened. Pour over squash. Bake stuffed squash at 350° for 25 minutes or until tender.

Serves 4.

Ninajean Rohlfs

My Grandma Bryan saw cooking as an adventure —an outlook that has been passed down through generations in our family. This recipe of hers was updated by my daughter, Rochelle, in 4-H, and won first place in a State Fair cooking demonstration. She went on to win a recipe contest with it when she was in college. An easy gourmet twist makes squash, a nutritious vegetable seldom served in many homes, a new favorite with the whole family. It's easy to make, yet special enough for a company meal. Fall is the prime season for Harvest Squash, but it's appealing any time of the year.

Crunchy Potato Balls

2 cups cooked, stiff mashed potatoes
2 cups cooked ham, finely chopped
1 cup (4-ounces) shredded cheddar or Swiss cheese
1/3 cup mayonnaise
1 egg, beaten
1 teaspoon prepared mustard
1/4 teaspoon pepper
3 to 4 Tablespoons all-purpose flour
1 3/4 cups crushed cornflakes

Combine potatoes, ham, cheese, mayonnaise, egg, mustard, and pepper in mixing bowl. Mix well; add enough flour to make a stiff mixture and then chill. Shape mixture into 1-inch balls (the size of a quarter). Roll in crushed cornflakes. Place balls on greased baking sheets. Bake at 350° for 25 to 30 minutes or until heated through. Serve hot.

Deb Holen

Potato Dumplings

2 cups potato flakes (do not use buds)
1 1/4 cups flour
1 teaspoon salt
1 egg
1 1/4 cups ice-cold water

Mix flakes, flour, and salt together. Add egg and water. Knead dough then form into logs. Drop into boiling water and cook for 5 minutes. They will float when they are done. Cool on wax paper for a few minutes. Serve warm. Makes 1 dozen dumplings.

Senator Russ and Jill Karpisek

The traditional Czech meal in Wilber is a duck-and-sauerkraut dinner that is just not complete without potato dumplings. Although they can be made with real mashed potatoes, here is a version that is just as good, less time-consuming, and even our children can make them. The only problem we have is not many make it to the dinner table, since everyone eats them as they come out of the kettle.

From 1900 through World War II, Lincoln, with the Governor's Residence at its center, was a hub of great social and political activity, due to its unique central geographical position in America's transportation network and its unique position in the country's political scene. In part, this was due to two prominent Nebraska politicians of that era, Populist William Jennings Bryan (Democratic nominee for president in 1896, 1902, and 1908) and Progressive George W. Norris (who served in Congress for forty years, 1902–1942)—their respective political movements of Populism and Progressivism were making waves throughout the country.

Aunt Anna's Baked Beans

1/2 pound bacon
1 medium onion, chopped
1 red bell pepper, diced
2 (20-ounce) cans pork and beans in tomato sauce
1 (8-ounce) can crushed pineapple, drained
1/2 cup ketchup
1/4 cup brown sugar
1 1/2 teaspoons dry mustard
1/2 teaspoon black pepper

Brown bacon, then add to it onion and bell pepper. After onion and pepper are cooked, add the rest of the ingredients and bake 35 to 45 minutes at 350°.

Nancy Enstrom

Pear Salad with Gorgonzola Dressing

4 cups salad greens and/or spinach leaves
1 (18-ounce) can pear halves, drained and cut into large dice
3 Tablespoons apple-cider vinegar
3 Tablespoons olive oil
1 Tablespoon honey
1/4 cup sour cream
1/4 cup plain yogurt
3/4 cup crumbled Gorgonzola cheese
3 Tablespoons walnuts

Divide greens between 4 plates and top with pears

In a medium mixing bowl, combine vinegar, oil, honey, sour cream, and yogurt. Fold in Gorgonzola. Drizzle dressing over salad. Garnish each plate with walnuts and serve.

Anita Wiechman

The original State Dining Room.

Main Dishes & Casseroles

The State Dining Room

The State Dining Room is used for numerous functions and features hand-cut chandeliers from Czechoslovakia. The silver set displayed in the room was used on the battleship *USS Nebraska*. The walls are covered with a Zuber mural from Paris entitled *Scenic America*.

The tables on either side of the windows in the State Dining Room are petticoat tables that include mirrors underneath them for use by ladies to discreetly check their skirts and be sure their ankles were not showing.

The formal place setting for the Residence includes a charger plate that features the Governor's Seal.

Main Dishes & Casseroles

Tastees

1/2 cup **Heinz Ketchup**
3 heaping teaspoons **Grey Poupon prepared mustard**
3 heaping teaspoons **Silver Spring Cream Style Horseradish**
3 teaspoons **Worcestershire sauce**
3 teaspoons **salt**
1/4 teaspoon **pepper**
5 pounds **very lean ground beef**
1 cup **finely chopped yellow onion**

Mix thoroughly the first six ingredients. Put ground beef in a large flat-bottom pan. Put the mixed seasonings on top of the beef. Use 1 cup water to rinse out seasoning bowl and add to beef mixture. Mix with a wooden spoon, then stir constantly over low heat gradually until mixture comes to a simmer. Let simmer for 25 minutes, stirring every few minutes to make sure that it does not stick to the bottom of the pan. Put a small amount of mustard on a bun along with 2 or 3 pickle slices. Spoon meat mixture on bun.

Former Governor Mike Johanns

Governors eat a lot of banquet food, so to sit down to a Tastee was just plain good eating! When I first moved into the Governor's Residence, I became aware that there were usually some pretty good leftovers in the refrigerator. So at night it was fun to go downstairs and raid the fridge. It didn't take long before the pounds started to creep on and hence the raids had to cease.

Main Dishes & Casseroles

This recipe was served to Governor Dave Heineman during elections in Wauneta, Nebraska.

Election Joes

10 pounds ground beef
2 1/2 cups chopped onion
3 1/2 cups ketchup
7 teaspoons mustard
7 teaspoons vinegar
4 teaspoons chili powder
7 teaspoons Worcestershire sauce
1/4 cup brown sugar
1/4 teaspoon garlic powder
3 packages sloppy joe seasoning mix
1 green pepper, chopped
3 (6-ounce) cans tomato paste
3 3/4 cups tomato juice

Brown the beef and onions together. Drain and place in a roaster oven and add the rest of the ingredients. Bring to a boil and then simmer to keep warm and serve.

Carol Maddux

Main Dishes & Casseroles

Pizza Burgers

1 1/4 pounds ground beef
1/4 cup chopped onion
Salt, to taste
1 teaspoon chili powder
1/4 teaspoon oregano
1 can tomato soup
1 can cream of mushroom soup
1 pound shredded mozzarella cheese

Brown hamburger and onions, cool. When cool, add salt, chili powder, oregano, tomato soup, mushroom soup, and shredded cheese. Spread 1 Tablespoon of mixture on half of a hamburger bun. Broil in oven broiler about 5 minutes or until bubbly. Serve warm.

Senator Carroll Burling

Senator and Mrs. Burling were youth directors in their community for a number of years and seemed to have a house full of hungry teenagers a great deal of the time. This is an easy recipe and one of their favorites. Served with juice or soda and chips, it makes everyone happy.

Main Dishes & Casseroles

Mexican Casserole

2 pounds ground beef
1 onion, diced
1 can enchilada sauce
1 can cream of mushroom soup
1 can pinto or chili beans
Corn chips
1 pound grated cheddar cheese

Brown beef and onion. Drain well. To this, add enchilada sauce, soup, and beans. Mix well. Layer in a 2-quart baking dish as follows:

1. Corn Chips
2. Beef mixture
3. 1 pound cheese

Bake at 350° for 25 to 30 minutes.

Kathy Fadschild

Taco Casserole

1 1/2 pounds hamburger
1 onion, chopped
1 (15-ounce) can tomato sauce
1 (1.25 ounces) package dry taco seasoning
1 can refrigerated crescent rolls
1 package corn chips
Shredded cheddar cheese
1 (8-ounce) carton sour cream

Brown together the hamburger and chopped onion, and drain excess grease. Add tomato sauce and dry taco seasoning. Press refrigerated crescent rolls into bottom of a 9 × 13-inch baking pan. Crush corn chips and put half of package on top of the crescent rolls. Add the meat sauce. Layer shredded cheddar cheese on top of this. Then top with sour cream. Top with the rest of the crushed corn chips. Bake 30 minutes in a 350° oven.

Bill Barrett

This taco casserole is always a favorite at church potlucks, especially with the kids.

This recipe was from a friend while we were living in Missoula, Montana. Our gardens were lush and produced abundantly, especially the zucchini. So ... we needed recipes, and this became our favorite. I have baked this for family gatherings, potlucks, and for friends in need; and many requests have been made for this recipe. Enjoy!

Zucchini-Hamburger Casserole

1 cup zucchini, diced
1 pound hamburger
1 small onion, chopped
1/2 cup instant rice, uncooked or 1 cup cooked rice
1/2 teaspoon garlic salt
1/2 teaspoon oregano
Pepper, to taste
1 1/2 cups cottage cheese
1 can cream of mushroom soup
1/2 can water
1 cup grated cheddar cheese (use more if you like)
Buttered bread crumbs or crushed potato chips

Brown the hamburger and onion; drain off fat. Add seasonings and rice. Place half of the zucchini in the bottom of a buttered 9 × 13-inch baking dish. Add hamburger mixture, cottage cheese, then the rest of the zucchini. Mix soup and milk, pour over the top. Sprinkle the cheese on top and then finish with the bread crumbs or potato chips as the top layer. Bake in a pre-heated 350° oven for 45 to 50 minutes.

Elizabeth Hofmann

Main Dishes & Casseroles

Overnight Casserole

1 pound ground beef
1 can tomato soup
1/4 cup celery, chopped
1/4 cup green pepper, chopped
1/4 cup onion, chopped
1 can cheddar cheese soup
1 cup dry macaroni
2 teaspoons sugar

Mix all together and place in a 9 × 9-inch pan. Cover with foil and refrigerate overnight. Bake in a 350° oven for 2 hours. Leave foil on for the first hour and then remove.

Lila Adams

This recipe is a favorite of the Don Adams family of Arapahoe, Nebraska. This family has a construction company that has been responsible for many roads throughout Nebraska.

Cabbage Casserole

1 pound hamburger
1 medium onion
1 small head cabbage, chopped
1 can cheddar cheese soup
2 cans refrigerated crescent rolls
Cheese slices (optional)

Brown hamburger with onion; drain. Add chopped cabbage and cook until transparent. Add cheddar cheese soup. In a greased 9 × 13-inch pan, roll out one can of crescent rolls to cover the bottom of pan and pinch together seams to seal. Put hamburger-cabbage mixture over crust. Cover with slices of cheese (cheddar or Velveeta). Put on second can of crescent rolls on top and pinch seams. Bake in a 350° oven until crust is brown.

Beverly Hansen

German Skillet Dinner

1 Tablespoon margarine
1 (16-ounce) can sauerkraut (do not drain)
1/2 cup rice
1/2 cup chopped onion
1 pound ground chuck or ground beef
1 1/4 teaspoons salt.
1/4 teaspoon pepper
1 (8-ounce) can tomato sauce

In a large skillet, heat margarine until melted. Spread sauerkraut evenly over margarine in skillet. Sprinkle on the rice, then the onion. Top with meat, salt, pepper, and the tomato sauce. Cover skillet; cook over low heat 25 to 30 minutes or until rice is tender.

Pat Wallmen

Talk about a quick supper in a busy farm wife's day! This all-inclusive recipe was a winner at harvest time when the children were in school at home. It came from Lila Papke's kitchen in Cortland about thirty years ago. This was a recipe shared by her in the 1980 edition of the Voice News *newspaper. Lila and her husband, Norval, remain very active in community affairs and the American Legion.*

Main Dishes & Casseroles

Tenderloin and Wild Rice Casserole

1 cup wild rice (soaked overnight)
2 cans cream of chicken soup
6 ounces evaporated milk
1 onion, chopped
2 cups celery, chopped
1 Tablespoon Worcestershire sauce
3 cups or more beef tenderloin, cubed and slightly browned
2 cans cream of mushroom soup
1 can of water
1/2 green pepper, chopped (optional)
1 medium can mushrooms, with liquid
1 teaspoon salt (optional)

Mix all ingredients, including liquid from mushrooms, and bake uncovered for 2 hours in a 350° oven, stirring twice. Baking time may vary between 2 to 3 hours.

Serves 6.

Nancy Whitaker

Pork Steak and Sauerkraut

2 or 4 pork steaks
1 (14 1/2-ounce) can sauerkraut
2 medium thinly sliced potatoes
1 medium sliced onion

Brown steaks in skillet. Put sauerkraut in casserole dish. Top with a layer of potatoes and a layer of onion. Place steaks on top. (Salt and pepper are optional.) Bake 2 hours at 350° with lid covering.

Sue Williams

This is a family favorite and is a special request whenever Roger's former college friend from the East Coast returns to hunt pheasants in the fall.

When the old Residence was demolished to make way for the new Residence, 1955–1957, its salvageable material and some effects were used in building and furnishing the new Residence. The State Historical Society also received a few items, and the remainder of the old Residence's furnishings were sold at auction on August 19, 1956. Nearly 300 items were sold, including the governor's oak desk and chair, five of six fireplaces, all lighting fixtures and chandeliers (except one), settees and chairs, end tables, bookshelves, a bedroom set, pictures, carpeting, and drapes. A citizen not able to attend the auction could write to Govenor Anderson for a momento—perhaps a piece of wallpaper or possibly a gavel carved from the wood of the old Residence.

Main Dishes & Casseroles

This recipe was given to me by my mother-in-law, Marie Novak Lorenz, who came to America in 1912 from Prague, Czechoslovakia, at the age of sixteen. She married William Lorenz, and they became dairy farmers in Orange County, New York, where they had a family of eleven children.

Flishcky (Czechoslovakian Casserole)

8 ounces wide egg noodles

Boil noodles as directed on package. (If you make your own noodles, cut into 1/2-inch squares.)

4 medium-size red potatoes (any potato usually works)

Cook potatoes in water to cover until tender. Cool, peel skin off, and dice.

2 cups ground cooked ham

Combine potatoes, ham, and noodles. Add about 1/4 teaspoon of black pepper. Put into a greased 8 × 8-inch baking dish. Drizzle 1/4 cup melted butter or margarine on top of mixture. Cover with foil and bake in a 350° oven for about 45 minutes. (Can be doubled and baked in a 9 × 13-inch baking dish.)

Serves 4.

Wilma L. Lorenz

Nelson's Creek Noodle Tuna Casserole

2 small onions, chopped
1 cup celery, chopped
2 cups water
2 cans cream of chicken soup, undiluted
2 (7-ounce) cans tuna, flaked
Salt and pepper, to taste
1 (12-ounce) package medium wide noodles, cooked
6 slices American cheese

Cook noodles according to package directions and drain. In 2 cups of water, cook the onion and celery until tender. Add soup, salt, pepper, and tuna, and simmer until hot. Combine cooked noodles and tuna mixture into a greased 4-quart baking dish. Top with cheese. Bake in a 350° oven until cheese melts.

Serves 6 to 8.

Senator Pete and Lori Pirsch

If you are looking for a casserole that is not difficult and time-consuming, this one fits the bill. Nelson's Creek is the subdivision in which we live in West Omaha. They tell us the creek was capped years ago when the land was first developed, so you can't see it. But it's a quaint name nonetheless, and our neighbors are great people. This recipe is a good one to make when any neighbor "pops by" for a visit.

This recipe was converted out of necessity. My two sons and their father were successful pheasant hunters—so successful that I needed to find a way to use up the wild game. Each day they hunted produced three to five pheasants. I needed a recipe that used a good deal of meat. Substituting pheasant for turkey was the solution. Ring-necked pheasants abound in Clay County. Their favorite refuge during hunting season is the nearby Roman L. Hruska Meat Animal Research Center (MARC), where they are protected. This recipe originally called for turkey but is a wonderful way to camouflage pheasant for those who say they do not care for pheasant. I have been making this hearty casserole for forty years and it never fails to draw a compliment.

Pheasant Dressing Casserole

4 cups chopped, cooked pheasant
4 cups bread crumbs
2 Tablespoons chopped onion
1/2 cup chopped celery
3/4 cup butter
1 1/2 teaspoons ground sage
1/2 cup broth
1/2 cup whole milk or evaporated milk
1 can cream of chicken soup
1 cup grated cheddar cheese

Cooking pheasant pieces in a pressure cooker makes the meat tender, moist, and easy to bone. Cooking in a stock pot also keeps it moist (save the broth). The breast and thigh meat is the best to use.

Cover the bottom of a buttered 9 × 13-inch baking dish with the 4 cups of pheasant. Sauté celery and onion in butter until onions are clear. Blend bread crumbs, onion, celery, butter, sage, and broth and spread mixture over pheasant. Whisk together the milk and cream of chicken soup. Pour over the dressing and pheasant. Sprinkle the cheese over the top. Bake in a 350° oven for 30 to 45 minutes.

Maryann Rolofson Thompson

Main Dishes & Casseroles

Creamed Chicken

1/3 cup butter
1 cup chicken stock
2 cups milk
3 cups diced, cooked chicken
1/2 cup flour
1 teaspoon salt
1/4 teaspoon celery salt
1 Tablespoon chopped celery

In a skillet, melt butter and add flour. When blended, add chicken stock and milk, stirring constantly on medium heat until thick. Add the salt, celery salt, and celery, cooking for 3 to 5 minutes.

Makes 8 servings.

Pat Wallman

This recipe comes from rural Gage County, circa 1930. I remember eating it as a child. We always had plenty of chicken on the farm, and we were eight people at every meal. It was a good way to stretch the meat and it was "healthy," even by today's standards. The gravy is already prepared and is delicious over mashed potatoes or toast. There were very seldom any leftovers.

Teda Meints

This recipe is wonderful to take to potluck church dinners. I have taken it several times and never came home with any leftovers since it is so well liked and easy.

Mexican Chicken

In a large skillet, sauté:

1 small onion, chopped
1 teaspoon salt
1/2 teaspoon pepper
1 Tablespoon cumin
4 Tablespoons butter

Add:

1 small can Swanson Chicken, drained
1 can mild green chilies, chopped
1 can cream of mushroom soup
1 (32-ounce) can diced tomatoes
1 (8-ounce) can tomato sauce

Line a 9 × 13-inch pan with taco-flavored Doritos. Pour above ingredients over the chips. Place 1 cup of grated cheddar cheese over the top. Bake in a 350° oven for 5 minutes, just to melt the cheese.

Pat and former State Senator Jim Jones

Main Dishes & Casseroles

Chicken Soufflé

10 slices of thin bread, with crusts removed
4 large chicken breasts, cooked (4 cups diced); tuna may be
  substituted
1/2 cup mayonnaise
1 can cream of celery soup
1 can cream of mushroom soup
1 to 2 ounces diced canned pimiento
10 slices sharp cheese (I use American singles)
1/3 cup butter
1 cup fresh mushrooms (or canned)
1 small can sliced water chestnuts
4 large eggs
2 cups milk
1 teaspoon salt
2 cups buttered bread crumbs

Line bottom of a 10 × 15-inch pan with 10 slices of bread. Top with 4 cups of diced chicken. Mix together the mayonnaise, celery soup, mushroom soup, and pimiento. Spread over chicken. Top with 10 slices of cheese. In a small skillet, melt butter and sauté mushrooms and water chestnuts for 5 minutes. Spread over cheese. Beat together the eggs, milk, and salt. Pour slowly over the entire casserole. (If using a 9 × 13-inch pan, you may want to use only 1 1/2 cups of milk so it doesn't boil over.) Top with buttered bread crumbs. Cover and refrigerate overnight. Bake in 350° oven for 1 1/2 hours, uncovered.

Lori Pankonin

Main Dishes & Casseroles

I have been a school superintendent for thirteen years. Prior to that, I was a pastor for eleven years. During that time, I was a youth pastor for four years at Tulsa Bible College in Tulsa, Oklahoma. In 1992, our drama group was performing Anne of Greene Gables *for three nights at a dinner theater. We were to serve over 200 people each night, and I was the head cook for the theater. An associate pastor on staff at the church was going to assist me in the preparation of the $25-a-plate dinners. He and I did some menu scouting a month in advance of the performance by eating at several upscale restaurants in Tulsa. We found a grilled chicken fettuccini Alfredo dish that was out of this world; we asked to meet*

continued on page 141

Grilled Chicken Fettuccine with Sun-Dried Tomatoes

1 pound boneless, skinless chicken breasts
  (marinated in low fat Italian dressing, grilled ahead of time, sliced into 1/4-inch strips, and set aside.)
1/2 ounce dried porcini (mushrooms)
4 ounces sun-dried tomatoes
1 cup boiling water

Put mushrooms and tomatoes in a bowl and pour boiling water over them. Set aside to soak for 30 minutes. Squeeze them dry and chop into small pieces.

7 Tablespoons butter
1 onion, finely diced
1/2 teaspoon hot red pepper flakes, or more to taste
2 cloves garlic
1/2 teaspoon dried rosemary
1 Tablespoon parsley, chopped
3/4 cup vodka (Russian or Polish)
1 cup of heavy cream

Heat butter in skillet, sauté onions; add the garlic, herbs, and vodka. Simmer for 20 minutes. Add the mushrooms, tomatoes, and cream and simmer for an additional 15 minutes. Season to taste with salt and pepper.

1 pound fettuccine
6 quarts of water
2 Tablespoons salt

Main Dishes & Casseroles

Bring water to a boil, add pasta, and cook for 8 to 10 minutes. Meanwhile, warm a large serving bowl. Drain the pasta well. Pour into serving bowl and top with cream sauce. Add 1 cup grated Parmesan cheese and mix thoroughly. Serve out on plates and place a few chicken strips of "warm" chicken on top of the fettuccine. Garnish with sprigs of fresh parsley.

Joe Sherwood

During the war-time administration of Republican Governor Dwight Griswold (1941–1947), the Residence was a major center of social activity, hosting frequent legislative lunches and dinners, as well as teas for visits by distinguished guests. When the Dwight Griswolds moved into the Residence, they brought their Labrador hunting dog, Buster. Being a faithful watchdog, Buster "clamped-down" one evening on the foot of former Governor Charles Bryan, according to Erma Griswold-Bomgardner. "It didn't faze Mr. Bryan at all," said the former First Lady. "He just looked down and said, 'Must have known I was a Democrat!'"

continued from page 140
with the chef, explained the cause, and requested the recipe. As you can guess, he refused to share his recipe. My partner and I embarked on a recipe search and assembled nearly 100 variations of Alfredo sauce, and together wrote one trying to match the flavors we tasted. We ate the dish at the restaurant three times, dissecting and evaluating it. We arranged a dinner for the pastoral staff and their spouses to present the original recipe that we wrote. We had never made the recipe prior to that occasion. The guests loved the dish, and we agreed that it was even better than the restaurant's. The dinner theater was a grand success, not only because the drama was great but because the **continued on page 142**

Main Dishes & Casseroles

continued from page 141

dinner was fabulous. I hope your family and guests will enjoy this as much as I do.

Easy Chicken/Stuffing Casserole

1 package Stove Top Stuffing Mix for chicken
4 boneless, skinless chicken breasts (about 1 1/4 pounds)
1 can condensed cream of mushroom soup
1/3 cup sour cream

Make stuffing according to package directions. Set aside. Place chicken in greased 2-quart baking dish. Mix soup and sour cream and pour over chicken. Spoon stuffing mixture evenly over chicken. Bake in a 350° oven for 35 to 40 minutes or until chicken is cooked. Preparation time is 10 minutes.

Makes 4 servings.

Lindsay Lewis

Governor Keith Neville (1917–1919) gave a more personal touch to the Residence. The Nevilles were the only occupants of the Residence to become parents while living there. Their youngest daughter, Irene, was born in the Residence on July 1, 1918.

Main Dishes & Casseroles

Brunch Pizza Squares

1 pound bulk pork sausage
1 (8-ounce) tube refrigerated crescent rolls
4 eggs
2 Tablespoons milk
1/8 teaspoon pepper
3/4 cup shredded cheddar cheese

In a skillet, cook sausage over medium heat until no longer pink; drain. Unroll crescent dough into a lightly greased 13 × 9-inch baking pan. Press dough 1/2 inch up the sides; seal seams. Sprinkle with sausage. In a bowl, beat the eggs, milk, and pepper; pour over sausage. Sprinkle with cheese.
Bake uncovered in a 400° oven for 15 minutes or until the crust is golden brown and the cheese is melted.

Ruth Epley

A friend sent this to me. It is great for a fun brunch item. It is also good to use for a group of girls after a slumber party. We serve the omelets for Easter brunch, as everyone can make their own.

Ziploc Omelet

This works great! Have guests write their name on a quart-size freezer bag with a permanent marker. Crack 2 eggs into the bag. Shake to combine them. Put out a variety of ingredients such as:

Shredded cheese
Diced ham
Diced onions
Chopped green peppers
Diced tomatoes
Cooked hash browns
Sliced mushrooms
Salsa

Each guest adds their choice of ingredients to their bag and shakes it. Make sure to get the air out of the bag and zip it closed. Place bags in rolling boiling water for exactly 13 minutes. (You can cook 6 to 8 omelets in a large pan.) Cut off top of bag and the omelet will roll out easily. Be prepared for everyone to be amazed!

This is nice to serve with fresh fruit and coffee cake. Everyone gets involved, and it is a great conversation piece. It creates an environment for people to mix and get acquainted if they have not previously met.

Judy Jensen

Main Dishes & Casseroles

Sausage, Egg and Cheese Casserole

12 eggs
1 cup diced sausage (I like Jimmy Dean Regular)
1/4 cup chopped green onion
3 Tablespoons butter
1 (3-ounce) can mushrooms, drained (optional)

Sauté sausage, onion, and mushrooms in butter. Whip eggs in bowl, pour into sausage mixture, and scramble over heat until set. Pour into a greased baking dish, a 9 × 9-inch or 8 × 8-inch square. (I use aluminum; no cleaning ... just throw away the pan.)

2 Tablespoons butter
2 Tablespoons flour
1 3/4 cups milk, or more
2 cups shredded American cheese, or more
Salt and pepper, to taste

Melt butter and blend in the flour. Add the milk and cheese. (I do mine in the microwave; works for me.) Pour over egg mixture and mix so cheese sauce blends into mixture.

4 Tablespoons butter
1/8 teaspoon paprika
2 1/4 cups soft bread crumbs (about 6 slices)

Combine the ingredients in a heated pan. Mix. Be careful not to burn. Sprinkle over egg-and-cheese mixture so as to form a crust. Freeze, or set in refrigerator if making the next morning. (If frozen to use at a later date, thaw completely in order to bake in only 30 minutes.) Bake in a 350° oven for 30

I received this recipe from my dear friend, Sandy Lundeen, of North Platte, Nebraska. My family has used this recipe for family brunches, breakfast parties, wedding showers, and, last but not least, on ski trips. It is by far the best "egg casserole" I have ever eaten. I'm in hopes that the ladies around our great state will enjoy it as much as I have. Please note that you can make it ahead, so it is very useful for any kind of gathering.

Main Dishes & Casseroles

minutes or until golden brown. Use a square baking dish for single recipe; use 9 × 13-inch baking dish for double recipe.

Garland L. Eskey

The Zuber mural in the State Dining room is similar to the mural Jackie Kennedy installed in the White House Entryway. Pictured in the Residence mural are New York Bay, West Point Military Academy (Governor Heineman is a graduate of West Point), Boston Harbor, Pipe-of-Peace Dance and Natural Land Bridge in Virginia, and Niagara Falls.

Breakfast Casserole

1 package regular-flavor pork sausage, cooked, crumbled, and
   drained
10 eggs, lightly beaten
3 cups milk
2 teaspoons dry mustard
2 cups shredded sharp cheddar cheese
6 cups cubed bread
1/2 teaspoon black pepper
1 teaspoon salt

Optional:

1/2 cup mushrooms, sliced
1/2 cup green onion, sliced

In a large mixing bowl, combine eggs, milk, mustard, salt, and pepper. Mix well. Distribute evenly half the bread cubes in a buttered 9 × 13-inch baking dish. Sprinkle half of the cheese, sausage, and other optional ingredients. Repeat layering using the bread, cheese, sausage, etc. Pour egg mixture evenly over entire casserole. Refrigerate overnight. Preheat oven to 325°. Bake uncovered for 55 to 60 minutes or until eggs are set. Tent with foil if top begins to brown too quickly.

Makes 6 large servings.

Vicki Bromm

I call it my "any-excuse-to-celebrate dish." It is very easy and great for a brunch.

This casserole was served on several occasions at a breakfast for senators in the State Capitol by a group of constituents.

Senator's Favorite Breakfast Casserole

1 stick margarine or butter (1/2 cup)
1 (32-ounce) package frozen hash browns (Southern style)
12 eggs
2 cups shredded cheddar cheese
2 cups chopped onion
1 cup milk
1 Tablespoon instant onion (optional)
1/2 teaspoon salt
1/2 teaspoon pepper
1/4 teaspoon dry mustard

Melt butter in a 9 × 13-inch baking dish. Pour 3/4 bag of hash browns in baking dish. In a bowl, beat the eggs and stir in the remaining ingredients. Pour over the hash browns. Sprinkle on the remaining hash browns. Dust with paprika. May be prepared and refrigerated overnight. Bake in preheated 350° oven for 1 hour.

Senator DiAnna Schimek

Main Dishes & Casseroles

Brunch Enchiladas

2 cups cubed, fully cooked ham
1/2 cup chopped green onions
10 (8-inch) flour tortillas
2 cups (8 ounces) shredded cheddar cheese, divided
1 Tablespoon all-purpose flour
2 cups half-and-half or milk
6 eggs, beaten
1/4 teaspoon salt (optional)

Combine ham and onions; place about 1/2 cup down the center of each tortilla. Top with 2 Tablespoons of cheese. Roll up and place, seam side down, in a greased 9 x13-inch baking dish. In a bowl, combine flour, cream, eggs, and salt until smooth. Pour over tortillas. Cover and refrigerate for 8 hours or overnight. Remove from refrigerator 30 minutes before baking. Cover with foil and bake in a 350° oven for 25 minutes. Uncover and bake for 10 minutes. Sprinkle with remaining cheese. Bake 3 minutes longer or until cheese is melted. Let stand for 10 minutes before serving.

Senator Mark Christensen

A good friend gave me this recipe thirty years ago. Just serve with fresh fruit and cinnamon rolls or coffee cake for a nice brunch. My family has always enjoyed this!

Bread/Cheese Soufflé

8 slices of day-old bread
1 1/2 pounds sharp cheese, grated
6 eggs, beaten
2 1/2 cups milk
1 rounded Tablespoon brown sugar
Paprika (sprinkle)
1 onion, finely minced
1/2 teaspoon dry mustard
1/2 teaspoon salt
Pepper, to taste
1/2 teaspoon Worcestershire sauce
Dash of red pepper flakes

Remove bread crusts and cut bread into small cubes. Mix all other ingredients together. Layer bread cubes and cheese mixture in a buttered 9 × 13-inch baking dish. Place covered in refrigerator overnight. Bake in a 300° oven for 1 hour. If desired, add chopped ham, mushrooms, or cooked chicken.

Former Senator LaVon Crosby

Cheese and Tomato Salad Pizza

Whole Wheat Pizza Dough

1 envelope dry yeast
3/4 cup lukewarm water, divided
1 cup all-purpose flour
3/4 cup whole-wheat flour
3/4 teaspoon salt
2 Tablespoons olive oil

Dissolve yeast in 1/4 cup lukewarm water. In a large bowl, combine flour, whole-wheat flour, and salt. Stir in 1/2 cup lukewarm water, olive oil, and yeast mixture. Combine until the mixture forms a rough dough; knead on a floured surface for 10 minutes or until it is smooth and satiny. Put dough in an oiled bowl, turning to coat. Let rise, covered, in a warm place for 1 hour or until doubled in bulk. (Or let the dough rise in the bowl, covered, in the refrigerator overnight.) Punch dough down. Make into desired shape.

Cheese and Tomato Pizza Topping

1 large shallot, thinly sliced (may use green onions)
4 large garlic cloves, thinly sliced
1 Tablespoon olive oil
1 Tablespoon chopped fresh parsley

Sauté shallots and garlic in olive oil until tender. Remove from heat and add the parsley.

When the summer garden is producing abundantly, this is a much-requested recipe in our household. The unique combination of flavors, colors, and texture makes it appealing to the eye, as well as pleasing to the palate. It is one of the first recipes our daughter requested when she moved away from home. The whole-wheat crust is actually great with regular pizza, too.

Main Dishes & Casseroles

Pizza

2/3 cup crumbled feta cheese
2/3 cup freshly grated Romano cheese
1 medium or large pizza crust, ready to bake (we use the whole-wheat
   crust recipe)

Sprinkle cheeses on top of crust leaving 3/4-inch border. Dot with shallot-and-garlic mixture. Bake in a preheated 425° oven until crust is golden brown and cheeses are melted, about 20 minutes.

Salad

4 large plum tomatoes, seeded and chopped
1/4 cup freshly grated romano cheese
1/2 cup fresh chopped parsley
1/4 cup olive oil
1 Tablespoon balsamic or red wine vinegar
1/4 cup fresh chopped basil
1 bell pepper, diced
1 whole chicken breast (or 2 individually frozen)
Salt and pepper, to taste

Sauté bell pepper until crisp-tender in a little olive oil. Cut chicken into strips and stir-fry (season with seasoning salt or salt and pepper) or grill whole chicken breasts and cut into small pieces after cooking). Combine all the salad ingredients and spread over pizza crust after it has been baked. Serve warm.

Lori Pankonin

Nana's Pizza Topping Sauce

1 pound cooked ground beef
1 clove garlic, chopped and browned in olive oil (some onion can also
   be browned at the same time, if desired)
1 (28-ounce can) crushed tomatoes
1/2 can (14 ounces) water
1 (6-ounce) can tomato paste
1 teaspoon salt
1/4 teaspoon pepper
1 Tablespoon oregano (fresh, chopped, or dried)

Pour in crushed tomatoes. Add 14 ounces water. Then add tomato paste, salt, pepper, and oregano. Prepare sauce and then add cooked ground beef. Cook all ingredients for 20 minutes on medium to low heat. Homemade dough is great, but the dough mix is just fine. Roll out dough and place in pizza pan. Add the sauce covering all of the dough. Sprinkle romano cheese over the sauce, adding any other ingredients. Put lots of mozzarella cheese on top. Preheat oven to 400°. Bake for 20 minutes. Remove pizza from hot pan and cool on a rack.

Donna Finocchiaro

Pop Over Pizza

2 pounds lean ground beef
1 small onion, chopped
3/4 teaspoon salt
3/4 teaspoon pepper
1 3/4 cups of water
1 (6-ounce) can tomato paste
1 (1.5-ounce) package of spaghetti sauce mix
8 ounces sliced mozzarella cheese

Preheat oven to 400°. Brown meat and onion with salt and pepper; drain off fat. Add spaghetti sauce mix, water, and tomato paste. Simmer for 10 minutes. Pour into a greased 9 × 13-inch pan. Top with sliced cheese.

Topping

2 large eggs
1 cup milk
1 Tablespoon oil
1/2 teaspoon salt
1 cup flour

Mix the first 4 ingredients and then add flour. Pour this over the meat and cheese. Bake for 35 minutes. Enjoy!

Paula Stromquist

Pizza Spaghetti

1 pound thin spaghetti, cooked
2 eggs, beaten
1/2 cup milk
3 cups mozzarella cheese, shredded
Garlic, to taste
3 pounds ground beef, browned
54 ounces spaghetti sauce (pepperoni or meat of choice)
3 cups mozzarella cheese, shredded

Beat eggs and milk together. Add 3 cups mozzarella cheese and garlic. Add spaghetti. Put mixture into 2 greased pans. Bake in a 375° oven for 15 minutes or until bubbly. Add spaghetti sauce to browned ground beef. Spread over baked spaghetti. Top with pepperoni and 3 cups mozzarella cheese. Bake in a 350° oven for 30 minutes. Cool before cutting into squares. You may use 1 pan and freeze 1 pan. If freezing a pan, don't do the second baking until you are ready.

Laurie Schepmann

Lasagna

1 (8-ounce) box lasagna noodles
1 pound ground beef
1 (23-ounce) jar Ragu Spaghetti Sauce
1/2 to 3/4 cup water
1 teaspoon salt
1/2 teaspoon sugar (optional)
1 pound small curd cottage cheese
3 cups shredded mozzarella cheese
1/2 cup grated Parmesan cheese

Brown ground beef and drain. Add spaghetti sauce, water, salt, and sugar. Simmer several minutes. In a 9 × 13-inch pan, layer:

1/3 of the sauce mixture
1/2 of the uncooked lasagna noodles
1 cup of cottage cheese
1 cup of shredded mozzarella cheese

Repeat layers, ending with the sauce and remaining mozzarella cheese. Cover with foil and bake at 350° for 55 to 60 minutes. Remove foil to brown; bake about 5 minutes more. Remove from oven and let stand for 10 minutes before serving.

Serves 12 to 14.

Beverly Hansen

'No Peek' Spaghetti

1 1/2 pounds ground beef
1 medium onion, chopped
2 cups tomato sauce
1/4 teaspoon garlic salt
4 Tablespoons sugar
1 cup water
1 cup spaghetti pieces (use the long kind and break it up)

Brown the beef and onion. Drain well. Combine tomato sauce, water, and seasonings and mix well. Add spaghetti pieces and beef mixture. Bake in a heavy skillet or large oven-proof baking dish with a tight-fitting lid. Bake in a 350° oven for 1 hour. Do not peek while baking!

Pattie Stuthman

The new Residence's architects were Selmer Solheim & Associates, Lincoln; the general contract went to the W. J. Broer Construction Company; Omahan J. B. Peacock of Orchard and Wilhelm Company was the interior decorator; and J. G. Welding was the landscape designer. The design, called modified Georgian Colonial by Solheim, was chosen from seven that had been presented to the State Building Commission. Solheim felt that his concept, based in American heritage, represented permanency and that a more contemporary building style would soon become dated.

Note on original recipe given to Tracy: "Love from the old lady next door to your grandparents, (signed) Margaret Darrow."

Fabulous Zucchini Pie

1/2 cup margarine
2 cups thinly sliced, peeled zucchini
1 cup coarsely chopped onion
1/2 cup chopped fresh parsley or 2 Tablespoons dried parsley flakes
1/2 teaspoon salt
1/2 teaspoon pepper
1/4 teaspoon garlic powder
1/4 teaspoon dried sweet basil leaves
1 egg, well beaten
1 cup (8 ounces) Muenster or mozzarella cheese, shredded
1 tube crescent rolls
1 teaspoon prepared mustard

Preheat oven to 375°. In a 10-inch skillet, cook zucchini and onion in margarine until tender (about 10 minutes). Stir in parsley and seasonings. In large bowl, blend eggs and cheese. Stir in cooked vegetable mix. Separate dough into 8 triangles. Place in an 8 × 12-inch pan or a 10-inch pie pan. Press over bottom and side to form crust. Spread crust with mustard. Pour vegetable mixture evenly into crust. Bake for 18 to 20 minutes or until inserted knife comes out clean. (During last 10 minutes of baking, cover crust with foil if necessary.) Let stand 5 to 10 minutes before serving. Cut into wedges and serve.

John and Tracy Wells

Eggplant Sicilian Caponata

1 medium eggplant
6 cups celery hearts, cut into 3/4-inch cubes
2 cups fresh onions, cut into 3/4-inch cubes
1 cup olive oil
3 large tomatoes
2 cups sliced mushrooms, canned or fresh
2 green peppers, cut into 3/4-inch cubes
2 cups sliced pimiento-stuffed green olives
1 large garlic clove, cut in half
2 quarts boiling water
Salt, to taste
Pepper, to taste

Cut eggplant into 1-inch slices and remove skin. Cut slices into 4 or 6 pieces, depending on the size of slice. Cooking in moderate heat, sauté eggplant in 1/2 cup olive oil until half cooked. Then add the cubed tomatoes.
(Note: To peel tomatoes, drop fresh tomatoes into boiling water long enough to permit skin to crack; peel tomatoes and cut into cubes.) In a separate pan using remaining olive oil, cook until half done the celery, onions, mushrooms, green pepper, olives, and garlic. Combine the eggplant and tomato mixture and continue cooking for 5 minutes on low heat. Add salt and pepper to taste; cool. Cover and store in refrigerator for 24 hours.

Lou Turco

A variation of this recipe was submitted by Peggy L. Green.

Summer Squash or Zucchini Casserole

5 or 6 cups summer squash or zucchini, sliced
1/4 cup chopped onion
1 can cream of chicken soup
1 cup sour cream
1 cup shredded carrots
1 small package herb stuffing mix
1/2 cup margarine or butter

Boil the zucchini and onion for about 5 minutes. Combine soup, sour cream, and carrots. Blend in vegetables. Mix stuffing mix and margarine. Place half of the stuffing mix in the bottom of a baking dish. Add soup mixture. Top with remaining stuffing. Bake in a 350° oven for 30 minutes.

Senator Carol Hudkins

Main Dishes & Casseroles

Vegetable Casserole Delight

1 can green beans, drained
1 can corn, drained
1 can cream of celery soup
1/2 cup shredded cheddar cheese
1/2 cup onion, finely chopped
1/2 cup sour cream
1/2 cup almonds or 1 can water chestnuts
Salt, to taste
Pepper, to taste
Ritz Crackers

Mix all together and place in a 2-quart baking dish. Top with 36 crushed Ritz crackers and then pour on 1 stick (1/2 cup) melted butter. Bake in a 350° oven for 40 minutes.

Kathy Christensen

Every December, Fort Robinson hosts an annual Christmas dinner. The dinner is based on an actual year that the Army served Christmas dinner to the troops stationed at the fort. Years ranged from 1874 to 1948, which are the years the fort was a military installation. Historical menus have been provided through the Historical Society, and the food is prepared from historical recipes researched by our staff. Menus, decorations, and entertainment for the dinners are prepared to be as close as possible to the year celebrated. In 2006, the year 1900 was celebrated. On the menu was "Potato Dressing," and this recipe is from The Heritage Cookbook 1975 *for the 200 guests that attended the dinner.*

Potato Dressing

In a skillet, cook:

3/4 cup chopped onion
1/4 cup chopped celery
1/4 cup butter

Cook until tender, but not brown.

Thoroughly combine:

2 cups mashed potatoes (2 medium)
1 1/2 cups soft bread crumbs
2 beaten eggs
2 Tablespoons snipped fresh parsley or 1 Tablespoon dried parsley
3/4 teaspoon salt
1/2 teaspoon dried marjoram, crushed
1/8 teaspoon pepper

Use to stuff poultry or bake covered in a 1-quart baking dish in a 375° oven for 45 minutes.

Makes 3 cups of dressing.

Michael Morava, Superintendent, Fort Robinson State Park

Scotch-Currant Dressing

8 cups bread crumbs
1/2 cup flour
1/2 teaspoon soda
3/4 cup butter
2 1/2 cups currants (plumped up in 2 cups hot water, drained)
2 teaspoons cinnamon
1 teaspoon nutmeg
1 teaspoon allspice
1 Tablespoon jelly or jam (any kind)

Mix ingredients; moisten with cream or milk. Bake in a 325° oven until done.

Josephine Mierendorf

This is a very old recipe from my grandmother, whose family came to the United States from Scotland and settled in the Bloomington and Franklin, Nebraska, area in the early 1870s. Our ancestors must have not thought much about calories! Today's cook would likely lighten up on the butter and definitely use milk. They stuffed turkey or chicken with this or baked it separately. It is more of a side dish and even can be used as a dessert-like bread pudding.

More than 18,000 people toured the new Residence during the March 15–16, 1958, open house. Appropriately, the first visitors were those by and for whom it was built, the citizens of Nebraska.

Main Dishes & Casseroles

Knip is pronounced with a hard k *and is said to be a German word meaning "head cheese." When hogs were butchered, it was said that "everything was used but the squeal." The hog head was scraped and cleaned, then boiled until the meat fell from the bones. Today we go to the supermarket and buy a beef roast and a pork roast. Our family believes that the secret to great flavor is to grind the allspice.*

My maternal grandmother, Florence Mathews, of Swedish descent made almost the same recipe and called it "head cheese." She placed the mixture in a clean tea towel and squeezed the grease out. Then it was placed in a crock with a plate and a heavy weight on it to flatten the

continued on page 165

Knip

4 pounds beef chuck roast
4 pounds pork roast
6 cups quick-cook oatmeal
4 teaspoons salt
1 teaspoon pepper
3/4 bottle of McCormick Whole Allspice

Put roasts in individual roasting pans and cover with water. Cook for 4 to 5 hours in a 350° oven until tender. Remove the meat and let cool. In a large bowl, grind the meats with a medium-fine blade. Combine the beef and pork broth, about 10 to 12 cups, and add the oatmeal. Do not cook the oatmeal mixture, just let it soak until the liquid is absorbed. It will have a "soupy" texture to it. Coarsely grind the allspice with a food processor or a Pampered Chef Food Chopper. Then combine the oatmeal mixture, ground meats, salt, pepper, and ground allspice. Stir and put into containers to freeze.

To serve:

Heat the mixture in a heavy skillet at a low to medium heat until warmed through and browned on the bottom. Serve with coarse-milled, hearty bread. Homemade bread is especially good with it. Some folks make patties and brown. This may be refrigerated up to 4 or 5 days.

Vicki Goings
Pam Gloy
Phyliss Nordhausen

Main Dishes & Casseroles

The tablecloth used in the State Dining Room was handstitched by the nuns of Notre Dame, and includes images of the Capitol and Notre Dame (close-up detail images below). The Zuber mural from Paris, *Scenic America*, covers the four walls of the room.

continued from page 164
mixture. This was then sliced and used for sandwiches. Others sliced and fried it.

My sister Pam and I remember eating knip and homemade bread when we were growing up on a farm in southwest Nebraska. It always seemed to stay with us better than any other breakfast. Pam made her first batch this winter and graciously shared it with all of us. We have to say it was still as good as it was some forty-five years ago.

Main Dishes & Casseroles

The original Formal Drawing Room, housing the French barometer.

Meats, Poultry & Seafood

The French Barometer

Since the original opening of the Governor's Residence, a French barometer has graced the fireplace of the house. As the renovation of the Residence was designed and completed, the French barometer was moved from the Formal Drawing Room to the Lower Conference Room.

The silver service displayed in the State Dining Room was used aboard the battleship *USS Nebraska* from 1908 until it was decommissioned in 1920.

Meats, Poultry & Seafood

Beef Fillet with Madeira Sauce

6 Tablespoons butter
1 fillet of beef (8–10 pounds)
Salt and pepper
2 cups Madeira Sauce

Preheat oven to 450°. Heat 4 tablespoons butter in shallow roasting pan. When melted, turn fillet in butter until meat is coated. Sprinkle with salt and pepper. Insert meat thermometer and place fillet in oven. Cook to desired doneness (medium-rare is best).

After meat is cooked, remove pan from oven and transfer beef to a carving board. Pour off most of fat from pan and pour in Madeira Sauce. Stir to dissolve brown particles. Swirl in remaining 2 tablespoons butter. Slice beef and serve sauce over it. Put extra sauce over it. Put remaining sauce in sauceboat. Serves 12.

Madeira Sauce

1 Tablespoon butter
4 large mushrooms, sliced
Salt and freshly ground pepper
2 Tablespoons finely chopped shallots
1/3 cup Madeira Wine
1 1/2 cups beef gravy (use any good canned gravy)

Heat butter in skillet and add mushrooms. Sprinkle with salt and ground pepper and cook until mushrooms give up their liquid. Add shallots and cook, stirring, until most of liquid evaporates. Add Madeira wine and cook

The beef fillet recipe is a tradition in our home for Christmas Eve. I have been making it for over thirty years and my family and friends love it. Our traditional Christmas Eve starts with church services at 5:30 and then we gather at our home at 7:00. I always request that everyone dress up for the evening because it is Christmas and a very special occasion. For the rest of the dinner, Ben makes oyster stew (a tradition in his home growing up), and I serve a tossed salad garnished with sliced pears and diced cranberries. I also make a mashed-potato casserole and serve fresh broccoli garnished with sliced, toasted almonds. Dessert is always something different every year. In the past, I have made
continued on page 170

Meats, Poultry & Seafood

continued from page 169

baked Alaska, cherries jubilee, Christmas cookies served with mint chip or peppermint stick ice cream, and Swedish cream topped with a raspberry sauce. We love Christmas and our traditional Christmas Eve dinner, and I hope you will enjoy making our favorite beef tenderloin recipe.

1 minute, then add gravy and simmer 15 minutes longer. Sauce may be made 1 day ahead. Makes 2 cups.

Former First Lady Diane Nelson

The alcoves in the State Dining Room are the perfect setting for the silver service (see photos page 168), which was used aboard the battleship USS Nebraska from 1908 until it was decommissioned in 1920. The service was brought to Nebraska at the request of Governor Sam McKelvie. The service originally contained 1,300 ounces of silver and included a punch bowl and ladle, eighteen cups, a centerpiece with attached candelabra, flower vase with pedestal, and a large tray to hold the punch bowl. Over the years, several pieces have disappeared.

Meats, Poultry & Seafood

Boeuf Bourguignon

6 ounces chunk of bacon
1 Tablespoon olive oil or cooking oil
1 pound lean stewing beef (rump pot roast), cut into 2-inch cubes
1 carrot, sliced
1 onion, sliced
1 teaspoon salt
1/4 teaspoon pepper
2 Tablespoons flour
3 cups red wine
2 to 3 cups brown beef stock, or canned beef bouillon
1 Tablespoon tomato paste
2 cloves mashed garlic
1/2 teaspoon thyme
Bay leaf, crumbled
Blanched bacon rind
18 to 24 small white onions, brown-braised in stock
1 pound quartered fresh mushrooms sautéed in butter

1. Remove rind, and cut bacon into "chunks." Simmer rind and bacon for 10 minutes in 1 1/2 quarts of water. Drain and dry.

2. Preheat oven to 450°.

3. Sauté the bacon in the oil over moderate heat for 2 to 3 minutes to brown lightly. Remove to a side dish with a slotted spoon. Set casserole aside. Re-heat until fat is almost smoking before you sauté the beef.

Meats, Poultry & Seafood

4. Dry the beef in paper towels; it will not brown if it is damp. Sauté it, a few pieces at a time, in the hot oil and bacon fat until nicely browned on all sides. Add it to the bacon.

5. In the same fat, brown the sliced vegetables. Pour out the sautéing fat.

6. Return the beef and bacon to the casserole and toss with the salt and pepper. Then sprinkle on the flour and toss again to coat the beef lightly with the flour. Set casserole uncovered in the middle position of the preheated oven for 4 minutes. Toss the meat and return to oven for 4 minutes more. (This browns the flour and covers the meat with a light crust.) Remove casserole, turn oven down to 325°.

7. Stir in the wine, and enough stock or bouillon so that the meat is barely covered. Add the tomato paste, garlic, herbs, and bacon rind. Bring to simmer on top of stove. Then cover the casserole and set in preheated oven. Regulate heat so liquid simmers very slowly for 3 to 4 hours. The meat is done when a fork pierces it easily.

8. While the beef is cooking, prepare the onions and mushrooms. Set them aside until needed. When the meat is tender, pour the contents of the casserole into a sieve set over a saucepan. Wash out the casserole and return the beef and bacon to it. Distribute the cooked onions and mushrooms over the meat. Skim fat off the sauce. Simmer sauce for a minute or two, skimming off additional fat as it rises. You should have about 2 1/2 cups of sauce thick enough to coat a spoon lightly. If too thin, boil it down rapidly. If too thick, mix a few Tablespoons of stock. Taste carefully for seasoning. Pour the sauce over the meat and vegetables.

This recipe can be prepared completely ahead, even a day in advance, and it only gains in flavor when reheated.

For immediate serving: Cover the casserole and simmer for 2 to 3 minutes, basting the meat and vegetables with the sauce several times. Serve in its casserole dish or arrange the stew on a platter surrounded with potatoes, noodles, or rice and decorated with parsley.

For later serving: When cold, cover and refrigerate. About 15 to 20 minutes before serving, bring to a simmer, cover, and simmer very slowly for 10 minutes, occasionally basting the meat and vegetables with the sauce.

Former Governor Kay A. Orr

Arthur Smith designed the silver service in the State Dining Room to depict Nebraska as it was becoming a state in the mid-1800s. It features the first territorial capitol building, Union Pacific Railroad, boats on the MIssouri River, agriculture, wildlife, Native Americans, a sod house, and a covered wagon

Originating in 1917, Omaha-based Omaha Steaks is a fifth-generation, family-owned company known nationwide for the finest in premium beef. From its humble beginnings as a customer butcher shop, the company is now recognized as America's largest direct-response marketer of premium quality beef and gourmet food gifts, including a complete line of pork, poultry, seafood, side dishes, appetizers, and desserts.

Omaha Steaks Famous Grilled Peppered Filet Mignon

4 Omaha Steaks filet mignons (7 ounces each)
1 Tablespoon Dijon mustard
3 Tablespoons freshly cracked black peppercorns
1 Tablespoon freshly cracked red peppercorns
1/2 Tablespoon kosher salt

Bring the steaks to room temperature. Brush both sides with the Dijon mustard. Combine the peppercorns and salt on a plate and roll the steaks in the mixture, pressing to coat each side well. Grill the steaks over direct medium-high heat for about 5 minutes per side for medium-rare, 6 to 7 minutes per side for medium, or to the desired doneness. Transfer to dinner plates and serve.

Omaha Steaks

Meats, Poultry & Seafood

Standing Rib Roast

4-rib standing rib roast (6 to 6 1/2 pounds, tied with kitchen string)
Salt and freshly ground pepper, to taste
1/4 cup chopped fresh thyme
1 cup dry red wine
1 cup beef stock

Let roast stand at room temperature for 1 hour. Position rack in lower third of oven; preheat to 450°. Generously season roast with salt, pepper, and thyme. Place roast, fat side up, on a rack in a large roasting pan and roast 20 minutes. Reduce heat to 350°; roast until a meat thermometer inserted into center of roast, away from the bone, registers 125 to 130°. For very rare to medium rare, about 1 1/2 hours more. Transfer to a carving board, cover loosely with foil, and let rest 15 minutes. Carve. Serves 8 to 10.

Senator Deb and Bruce Fischer

Spring is a busy time in ranching country in the Nebraska Sandhills with calving and brandings. This prime rib is easy to prepare and delicious.

Baked Steak

1 round steak (tenderized)
Oil to brown the steak
2 to 3 Tablespoons flour
1 can cream of mushroom soup
Milk

Heat oil. Flour the meat and put into oil. Brown both sides and put into 9 × 13-inch pan. Add 2 to 3 Tablespoons flour to the oil left in the pan and add milk when the flour is all mixed in. When the gravy thickens, add the mushroom soup and you may need to add more milk depending on how thick you like the gravy. Pour over the meat and move the meat around so that the gravy is underneath the meat. Bake 1 hour and serve over mashed potatoes or rice.

I hope you enjoy this as much as our family does.

Keron Bailey

Zobel's Café German Steak

4 minute steaks
2 bacon slices (raw)
2 dill pickle spears
3/4 cup flour seasoned with salt and pepper for coating

Sauce

1/4 cup ketchup
1/2 cup water
1 teaspoon Worcestershire sauce
1/4 teaspoon garlic powder

Cut steaks into 2 × 4 pieces. Lay half of a slice of bacon on each piece of steak and half of a dill pickle spear on bacon. Roll up and secure with toothpicks. Dip in flour seasoned with salt and pepper. Sear in hot skillet with butter. Place in covered casserole dish and cover with sauce. Bake 45 minutes at 350°. Serves 4.

Marlene Bunger Sanders

This is an original recipe from Zobel's Café in Hildreth, Nebraska, from the early 1950s.

Meats, Poultry & Seafood

This recipe was one of my mother's recipes. It is easy to prepare and tastes great with mashed potatoes since the juice thickens nicely as a sauce. Another meal that is better the next day.

Swiss Steak

1 round steak, tenderized, or you may use cubed steak
1 large onion, sliced
5 to 6 stalks of celery
Green pepper, thinly sliced
2 large cans tomatoes

Roll steak in seasoned flour and brown. Sauté onions, green peppers, and celery lightly and place on top of steak. Pour tomatoes over steak. Cover with foil and bake 1 to 1 1/2 hours at 350°. About 10 minutes before serving, pour on 1 can of mixed peas and carrots, undrained. Serve with mashed potatoes, vegetables, and hot bread.

Judy Jansen

The cabinetry on either side of the fireplace in the lower level conference room was designed to contain twenty-six place settings of Lennox china, featuring Nebraska wildflowers, that was donated by the Nebraska Chapter of the World Organization of China Painters.

Meats, Poultry & Seafood

Jan's 'Famous Dave's' Baby Back Ribs

3 racks pork baby back ribs (do not use spare ribs)

Jan's Magic Rub

1/4 cup ground coriander
1/4 cup paprika
1/4 cup kosher salt
3 Tablespoons ground cumin
3 Tablespoons dried thyme
1 1/2 Tablespoons dry mustard
1 1/2 Tablespoons garlic powder
3/4 teaspoon white pepper
3/4 teaspoon allspice
3/4 teaspoon cayenne pepper

Mix together in a small bowl. (Can be kept in a tightly closed jar for up to 3 months.)

Orange-Chipotle Barbecue Sauce

Sauté in 2 Tablespoons vegetable oil:

1 cup yellow onion, finely chopped

Add and simmer for 30 minutes:

2 Tablespoons garlic, minced
1 cup ketchup
1 cup orange marmalade

I started serving these ribs to farmers at my husband's annual field day several years ago. They were such a hit that I make them every year by request. Many of the farmers in attendance have attended RibFest in Lincoln and tell me that these are, in their opinion, better-tasting, fall-off-the-bone ribs than any they've had before. Each year, I prepare more than the year before (thirty-six racks in 2006), and there are never any left at the end of the lunch.

Meats, Poultry & Seafood

3/4 cup apple cider vinegar
1/2 cup brown sugar
1/4 cup Dijon mustard
1/4 cup lime juice
3 chipotle peppers

Off heat, stir in:

1/2 cup fresh cilantro, chopped

Preheat oven to 275°. Remove the thin skin from the bone side of the ribs by pulling with a paper towel. Rub 2 Tablespoons of the special rub on each side of the racks. Place on a large baking sheet (with sides) bone side down. Allow to sit for up to 2 hours (or overnight in the refrigerator covered with plastic wrap). Cover the baking sheet with heavy-duty aluminum foil so no steam can escape. Bake 2 to 2 1/2 hours or until the meat is beginning to pull away from the ends of the ribs.

Preheat gas grill on high or prepare charcoal grill. Clean grates thoroughly and lightly oil them. Reduce heat to medium. Grill the racks, meaty side down, for 7 minutes. Turn and brush with the Orange-Chipotle Barbecue Sauce. Grill an additional 7 minutes. Turn and brush again. Watch carefully as the sauce can burn easily.

Remove, cut between the ribs, and serve with additional sauce and lots of napkins. Enjoy!

Former Senator Jan McKenzie

Meats, Poultry & Seafood

The Perfectly Cooked Steak

4 to 5 pounds of porterhouse or bone-in rib-eye steak, 1 1/2 to 2 inches thick
Sea salt
Freshly ground pepper

Heat oven to 450°. On the stove top, heat a large, dry skillet until it is very hot. Season the steak well with salt and pepper and sear for 2 or 3 minutes on each side until it has a dark crust. Place skillet in preheated oven for about 14 minutes for a 1 1/2-inch steak. Cook to between rare and medium-rare because residual heat will continue cooking the meat while it is resting. To test for doneness, press your finger to the meat; it should yield to the touch but not be too soft. Don't use a thermometer as it will pierce the meat and allow the juices to run out. Rest steak for at least 5 minutes before slicing and serving. Makes 4 servings.

Active preparation time: 5 minutes
Cooking time: About 20 minutes for rare and medium-rare

Secretary of State John and Carol Gale

Having lived in North Platte, Lincoln County, for twenty-nine years, I have enjoyed the rich blend of history in that area, from the far horizons of Sandhills ranching to the immense trackage of the Union Pacific classification yards to the irrigated cornfields of the Platte River Valley. Buffalo Bill's Scout's Rest Ranch and the Nebraskaland Days annual western celebration were also a part of that history. Eating good, corn-fed Nebraska steaks was an established tradition. You could find great steaks from the Canteen Grill in North Platte to Butch's in Hershey to Ole's in Paxton, and other fine restaurants as well.

Senator Ernie Chambers
continued on page 182

Meats, Poultry & Seafood

This recipe came from a friend of mine. My family and friends love it. It is great to prepare for a group whose members will not be eating at the same time because it only gets better as it sets. If there are leftovers, they may be frozen and reheated.

continued from page 181
once dubbed me "Secretary of Steak" because of my long association with the Brand Committee. A good friend of ours in North Platte, Dr. Byron Barksdale, introduced us to this recipe.

Barbecue Beef

3 to 4 pounds lean beef roast
1 onion, chopped
2 Tablespoons butter
2 Tablespoons vinegar
2 Tablespoons brown sugar
4 Tablespoons lemon juice
1 small bottle ketchup
3 Tablespoons Worcestershire sauce
1 teaspoon mustard
1/2 cup celery, chopped

Cut beef into small pieces. Barely cover with water and bring to a boil. Add all remaining ingredients and simmer uncovered 3 to 4 hours. Mash with a potato masher and serve on sesame seed buns.

Judy Jansen

Meats, Poultry & Seafood

Rouladen und Sosse
(Rolled and Stuffed Braised Beef)

8 thin slices top round of beef (about 6 to 7 ounces each)
1/2 cup prepared mustard
8 strips of lean bacon
1 jar dill pickles, sliced lengthwise
1 large onion, chopped
1 1/2 teaspoons dried marjoram
8 Tablespoons (1 stick) unsalted butter
2 medium carrots, peeled and cut lengthwise and in half
4 large mushrooms, halved (or 1 can mushroom pieces)
1 medium onion, halved
6 Tablespoons all-purpose flour
1 quart beef broth
2 bay leaves

Spread each piece of beef with 1 Tablespoon mustard. Place a strip of bacon lengthwise on each piece, also 1 pickle spear and 1 teaspoon chopped onions. Sprinkle marjoram on top. Roll up and tie with kitchen twine in 3 places. (At this time the rolls could be refrigerated 1 to 2 days until ready to complete recipe, if desired.) In a deep Dutch oven, melt butter over medium heat. Add beef rolls, 3 at a time, and sauté until brown, about 2 1/2 minutes on each side. Do not scorch. Transfer beef rolls to a plate. Add mushrooms, carrots, and onion halves; sauté over medium heat until lightly browned. Gradually whisk in flour; continue stirring until flour is lightly browned. Slowly stir in broth. Add bay leaves. Heat to boiling, reduce heat, and add rouladen (beef rolls). Cover and simmer for 1 hour or more. Preheat oven to 350°. Transfer

Rouladen is great with mashed potatoes and a sauerkraut dish. The gravy is delicious over everything. This has become our traditional Christmas Day dinner. Of course, we make it at other times too, such as when Mom and Dad visit.

Meats, Poultry & Seafood

rouladen and carrots to an oven-safe serving dish and remove twine, keeping rolls intact. Strain gravy; pour some over rouladen and carrots. Heat for 30 minutes. While in oven, thicken gravy. Serves 6 to 8. Leftovers are tasty.

Deb (Hohnstein) Schark

Governor and Mrs. Nelson presented one cup, enclosed in a large glass case in the State Dining Room, to the nuclear submarine USS Nebraska at its commissioning on July 10, 1993.

Sweet and Sour Meatballs

1 pound hamburger
1/2 cup bread crumbs
1/4 teaspoon thyme
1 teaspoon garlic salt
1 teaspoon onion flakes
1 Tablespoon parsley flakes
1/2 teaspoon salt
1/4 teaspoon pepper

Sauce

1 Tablespoon soy sauce
6 Tablespoons water
3 Tablespoons cornstarch
3 Tablespoons vinegar
1/2 cup sugar
1 green pepper, cut into strips
1 (9-ounce) can pineapple chunks

Mix and shape first 8 ingredients into small meatballs. Sauté until done.

Mix the next 5 ingredients for sauce and stir until thick. Add meatballs, pineapple, and green pepper and heat through.

Senator Carol and Larry Hudkins

Do you need a quick and easy main dish for a potluck dinner? This is one everyone loves! After it is done, put in the Crock-Pot to stay warm. The pineapple and the green pepper strips add spots of color, and the spices in the meatballs give them a je ne sais quoi *taste. They are almost as good cold.*

Herbert J. Duis from Gothenburg served in the Legislature from 1969 to 1980. While campaigning, he distributed cards with this family recipe on the back.

Swedish Meatballs

2 pounds ground round steak
1 pound ground pork steak
2 eggs, beaten
1 cup mashed potatoes
1 cup dry bread crumbs
1 teaspoon brown sugar
1 1/2 teaspoons salt
1/2 teaspoon pepper
1/2 teaspoon ginger
1/2 teaspoon nutmeg
1/2 teaspoon cloves
1/2 teaspoon allspice
1 cup milk
1 pint cream

Mix first 13 ingredients to make a soft mixture that can barely be handled. Form into balls and roll in flour. Fry on all sides in a small amount of hot fat until brown. Pour 1 pint of cream over the meatballs. Cover and let simmer until the meat is tender, about 30 minutes. The cream makes delicious gravy.

Senator John and Janet Wightman

Meats, Poultry & Seafood

Aunt Tina's Meatballs

2 pounds ground beef
1 clove of garlic, chopped
1/3 cup bread crumbs
1 cup grated cheese (pepato, pesorino, or romano)
5 eggs
2 teaspoons salt
2 teaspoons pepper
Sauce of your choice

Mix together all ingredients except the ground beef. Add it last and blend it together by hand. If it's too firm, add a splash of water or another egg. Form into balls and gently drop into the bubbling sauce. Let cook about 45 minutes. I like to make it all the day ahead so the ingredients can blend. Two pounds of ground beef will make about 20 to 22 meatballs.

Donna Finocchiaro

It was tradition. We arrived at Nana's house on Sunday by noon—no later! Still wearing her hat from church, Nana filled the pasta pot with water for boiling. The grandchildren liked the mostaccoli best because they could keep it on their forks. The rich, red sauce bubbled on the stove and all the meatballs, sausage, and pieces of roast rolled about as it simmered. Wonderful aromas filled the kitchen and offered a warm welcome. Aunt Tina and her father announced their arrival with a short honk of the car horn. Aunt Tina was Nana's sister. She always made the salad. Their father was in his nineties and he knew all the great-grandchildren by name. He was dearly loved. His presence added the fourth generation to the weekly **continued on page 188**

Meats, Poultry & Seafood

continued from page 187

gathering. The dining-room table was colorful with the Italian flowered tablecloth and napkins. Paper napkins had no place at the table. The staples were these: Italian bread, olive oil (no butter!), grated pepato cheese, and a cruet of wine vinegar. Fresh fruit, nuts, and sweets followed for dessert. It was an event. I watched and learned and came to the realization that most Italian women alter a recipe to make it their own, especially spaghetti sauces. As with this recipe, Nana loved to add chopped parsley and a bit more garlic to her meatballs. Tina never added parsley. It's all OK, so experiment!

Meatballs with Sauce

3 pounds of ground beef
1 can evaporated milk
2 cups quick oatmeal
2 eggs
1/3 teaspoon garlic powder
1 cup onion, chopped (optional)
2 teaspoons salt
1/2 teaspoon pepper
2 teaspoons chili powder

Sauce

2 cups ketchup
1 1/2 cups brown sugar
2 Tablespoons Liquid Smoke
1/2 teaspoon garlic powder
1/2 cup onion, chopped

Combine first 9 ingredients and form into 1-inch balls. Combine sauce ingredients and pour over meatballs. Bake at 350° for 1 hour. They can be made the day before and refrigerated.

Jo Lamb

Italian Meatballs

1 1/2 pounds of ground beef, some fat content for tenderness
2 eggs
1 to 2 small garlic cloves, minced finely
1 to 2 Tablespoons parsley leaves
1 cup bread crumbs (broken Italian bread, if you have it)
1/2 cup Parmesan cheese
Salt and pepper to taste

Mix all together; shape into balls and fry slowly in hot oil, turning frequently until done. Serve with homemade tomato sauce.

Janet Caldararo

The remodeling has made the former basement of the Residence into a lower level, including a conference room. The ceiling was raised and architectural columns and detailed moldings were added, and the original painted cinder-block walls and massive brick fireplace have been replaced with an aesthetically pleasing and versatile space.

As a young newlywed of Swedish descent who had married a nice Italian boy, I quickly learned the value of "Sunday gravy"! (And not the roast-beef-and-brown-gravy kind.) Fortunately, I had a wonderful mother-in-law who was willing to share her recipe for the heart and soul of the tomato sauce: the meatball. The recipe itself is extremely simple; however, during my early married years living in New York and visiting Italian relatives on both sides of the family, I came to realize that not all meatballs are created equal. During one visit to my husband's uncle's home, my mother-in-law and Aunt Winnie proceeded to make the "meat-a-ballas." These two lovely ladies of the house that day had two very different ideas on **continued on page 190**

Meats, Poultry & Seafood

Many years ago, we were invited to a dinner party at my father's twin sister's home, Eleanor Green Weblemoe. Another guest, Mitch Tavlin, locally known for his collection of world-famous wines, served the appropriate wine at each course. A memorable evening of good company, great food, and very fine wine.

continued from page 189

how to proceed. It was a cordial discussion as the meatballs were being constructed, yet serious and tense. Should the meatballs be big or little, round or triangular, crispy or not, in the sauce or out, etc., etc., etc.! Both ladies were excellent cooks and very used to being right. I am sure the meatballs met everyone's mouth in fine shape, but it **continued on page 191**

Company Meatloaf

1 cup cracker crumbs
1 1/2 pounds ground beef
1 (6-ounce) can tomato paste
2 eggs, beaten
1 cup green pepper, chopped
1 cup onion, chopped
3/4 teaspoon salt
1/8 teaspoon pepper
1 1/2 cups small curd cottage cheese
4 ounces canned mushroom pieces, drained
1 teaspoon parsley, chopped

Combine the first 8 ingredients except 1/2 cup of the cracker crumbs. Pat half of the meat mixture into an 8-inch square baking dish.

Mix the remaining 1/2 cup of cracker crumbs with the cottage cheese, mushrooms, and parsley. Spread over the meat mixture.

Top with remaining meat mixture. Bake at 350° for 1 hour. Let stand 10 minutes.

Peggy L Green

Meats, Poultry & Seafood

Best-Ever Meatloaf

1 1/2 pounds ground beef
1/4 cup chopped onion
1/4 teaspoon pepper
3/4 cup milk
3/4 cup quick oats
1 1/2 teaspoons salt
1 large egg, beaten
3/4 cup bread crumbs

Sauce

1/3 cup ketchup
2 Tablespoons brown sugar
1 Tablespoon mustard

Combine all meatloaf ingredients and mix thoroughly. Pack firmly into a greased loaf pan. Combine the sauce ingredients in a saucepan and cook until bubbly. Pour over the meat mixture. Bake at 350° for 1 hour.

Clara Loftus

continued from page 190
does prove that there really is a great meatball debate out there just waiting to be settled. For my money, this basic recipe will set the table for final resolution. Try and judge it yourselves.

Meats, Poultry & Seafood

Frikadeller (*Danish meatball*) *is a staple of the Scandinavian Smorgasbord at Dana College's annual Sights and Sounds of Christmas celebration. For more than thirty years, Sights and Sounds has brought thousands to the campus each December for concerts, programs, and food centered around Scandinavian Christmas traditions. This* frikadeller *recipe is from Denmark native Bodil (Strøm) Johnson, a 1961 graduate of Dana College and former Danish teacher.*

Frikadeller (Danish Meat Patties)

1 pound lean ground beef
1/2 pound ground pork
1/4 cup flour
1 teaspoon salt
1/2 teaspoon pepper
1 onion, grated
2 eggs
1 cup milk
Margarine (for frying)

Mix meats in large bowl with flour, salt, pepper, and onion. Add eggs, one at a time, then the milk. Mix well by hand. Shape the mixture into oblongs, 4 inches long, 2 inches wide, and 1 1/2 inches thick. Fry in margarine in heavy skillet for about 45 minutes, turning several times.

Bodil Strøm Johnson

Meats, Poultry & Seafood

Cajun Burgers

1 pound ground beef
2 teaspoons garlic salt
2 teaspoons ground Hungarian paprika
1 teaspoon dried basil leaves
1 teaspoon dry mustard
1 teaspoon ground thyme
1/2 teaspoon ground red pepper
1/2 teaspoon freshly ground black pepper
1 medium sliced onion, separated into rings
Sour cream
4 hamburger buns

Divide ground beef into 4 equal portions and form into patties. Combine garlic salt, paprika, basil, mustard, thyme, and ground red and black pepper into a bowl. Press seasoning mixture evenly into both sides of the patties. Meanwhile, heat a large, heavy nonstick frying pan over medium heat for 5 minutes. Cook patties approximately 6 minutes, turning once. Remove patties from heat; keep warm. Quickly cook and stir onion rings at high heat in meat juices until tender. Spread sour cream on bun and top with onions.

Former Secretary of State Allen Beermann

This recipe was entered into a celebrity cook-off in 1988 at the Nebraska State Fair.

Meats, Poultry & Seafood

Mediterranean Lamb Shanks

1 Tablespoon dried oregano, crushed
4 cloves garlic, minced
4 meaty lamb shanks (3 1/2 to 4 pounds)
1 (14 1/2-ounce) can garbanzo beans, rinsed and drained
1 (14 1/2-ounce) can diced tomatoes, undrained
1/2 cup chopped onion
2 Tablespoons lemon juice
1/2 teaspoon ground allspice
7 cups chopped fresh spinach
1/2 cup plain yogurt
1/4 cup chopped cucumber
1 Tablespoon fresh mint, snipped
Salt and pepper, as desired

In a small bowl, combine oregano, garlic, and 1/4 teaspoon salt. Rub mixture into meat with your fingers.

In a 4 1/2- to 6-quart slow cooker, combine garbanzo beans, tomatoes, onion, lemon juice, allspice, and 1/2 teaspoon ground black pepper. Place meat on top of bean mixture. Cover; cook on low-heat setting for 7 to 9 hours (or on higher heat setting for 3 1/2 to 4 1/2 hours). Remove meat from cooker; keep warm. Stir spinach into garbanzo mixture. Serve lamb shanks over garbanzo mixture. In a small bowl, combine the yogurt, cucumber, and mint. Top each serving with some of the yogurt mixture. Makes 4 servings.

Jane Oligmueller

Veal Oscar

4 3/4-inch veal tenderloin
2 Tablespoons butter
Salt and pepper to taste
8 tender asparagus spears
8 ounces crab meat, leg or lump
1 cup hollandaise or Bernaise sauce

Brown veal in butter in large skillet over high heat for 6 to 8 minutes or until done to taste, turning once. Remove to warm serving plate; sprinkle with salt and pepper to taste. Steam asparagus until crisp-tender. Crab may be warmed over steamed asparagus.

Assembly: Top each veal tenderloin with 2 asparagus spears, 2 ounces crab meat, and 2 ounces of hollandaise or Bernaise sauce. Serves 4.

Jane Oligmueller

This is probably my favorite dish! I first tasted it at Tony & Luigi's, a wonderful Italian steakhouse in Lincoln in the '80s. I serve it with a mixed green salad, a crusty loaf of bread ... and tiramisu for dessert. Enjoy!

Meats, Poultry & Seafood

I inherited the recipe from my former sister-in-law, who served it to us one Sunday for dinner. We loved it and have since prepared it numerous times for our family. It is definitely a favorite for all of us. I usually serve it with whipped or scalloped potatoes and a tossed salad.

A variation of this recipe was submitted by Lois Holen using 2 cups bread crumbs (replacing the 3 cups crushed graham crackers) and 1 cup milk (replacing the 2 cups milk). Ms. Holen noted that Phelps County was settled by Swedish immigrants and that this recipe is made in homes and gatherings throughout Phelps County.

Ham Balls

1 1/4 pounds ground ham
1 pound ground pork
1/2 pound ground beef
2 eggs
3 cups crushed graham crackers
2 cups milk

Sauce

1 1/2 cups brown sugar
1/2 cup water
1/2 cup vinegar
2 1/2 teaspoons mustard

Combine first 6 ingredients and mix well. (I usually prepare the mixture earlier in the day, storing it in the refrigerator. Then 2 hours before we would like to eat, I start the shaping process. The shaping is done with a spoon or can be done with your hands.) Form into balls the size of ping-pong balls. Put balls into buttered baking dish. Mix sauce ingredients together and pour the sauce over ham balls. Cover with foil and bake at 350° for 40 minutes. Halfway through the baking, you will want to remove the foil and scoop up the sauce and pour over the ham balls to let it all soak in. Two hours later, once they are done, it is time to enjoy. The sauce is so yummy, you will want to make sure you scoop some up to pour over the ham balls on your plate. Serves 12 or more.

Joann Schlapfer

Pork Chili

4 pounds pork roast, cubed into 1/4- to 1/2-inch pieces
1/8 cup oil
Salt, pepper, and garlic to taste
1 cup water
1 (22-ounce) can whole tomatoes
1 small can peeled jalapeños
1 clove crushed garlic
1 small chopped onion
Salt and pepper to taste

Trim away fat from pork. Brown pork in oil. Cook until done. Simmer until most of the juice is gone. Pour off any fat. Then add salt, garlic, and onions to taste. Add water and simmer, covered. In a blender, combine tomatoes, jalapeños, garlic, onion, salt, and pepper. Blend for a fairly chunky consistency. Pour into pork meat and simmer until heated through (about 10 minutes). Add water if more juice is desired. Add more tomatoes if it is too spicy or more jalapeños if not spicy enough.

Angie Estrada and Cecelia Sanchez

We make this pork chili because it is very good as a meal or with refried beans, rice or vermicelli, fried potatoes, and tortillas. We also use pork chili to smother enchiladas or burritos. It can be eaten a variety of ways.

Meats, Poultry & Seafood

Sun-Dried Tomato Pesto Stuffed Pork

Cooking spray
2 1/2 pounds pork tenderloin
1 cup prepared sun-dried tomato pesto
Salt
Ground black pepper
1/4 cup balsamic vinegar
2 Tablespoons prepared honey mustard
2 Tablespoons chopped fresh thyme leaves
2 cups quick-cooking rice, prepared according to package directions

Preheat oven to 400°. Coat shallow roasting pan with cooking spray.

Using a sharp knife, cut pork lengthwise 3/4 way through. Place in a prepared pan, spread sun-dried tomato pesto in incision. Fold pork back in half and use metal or wooden skewer to close seam. Season with salt and pepper.

Mix vinegar, honey mustard, and thyme. Spoon mixture over pork.

Roast 45 minutes until instant thermometer reads 155°. Let pork rest for at least 10 minutes before slicing crosswise into 1-inch thick slices. Serve with rice.

Anita Wiechman

Artichoke-Chicken Mélange

4 whole chicken breasts, boned and skinned
1/4 cup oil
3 carrots, cut into 2-inch julienned pieces
1/2 pound fresh mushrooms, halved
1 (14-ounce) can artichoke hearts, drained and halved
1/2 cup chopped green onion
1/2 cup sliced water chestnuts
1/8 teaspoon whole thyme
1/2 teaspoon salt
1/8 teaspoon pepper
2 cups chicken broth
2 Tablespoons cornstarch

Brown chicken in oil in large skillet. Add carrots; cover and simmer for 5 minutes. Add mushrooms, artichoke hearts, onions, water chestnuts, thyme, salt, and pepper; cover and simmer for 10 minutes. Combine broth and cornstarch in saucepan. Cook over medium heat, stirring constantly until thickened. Place chicken and vegetables in a greased 13 × 9 × 2–inch baking dish. Pour sauce over chicken and bake at 375° for 45 minutes. Baste chicken occasionally with pan drippings. Serves 6.

We add extra artichokes and water chestnuts because we love them. Perfect with a salad and crusty bread or garlic bread.

Deb (Hohnstein) Schark

Meats, Poultry & Seafood

Chicken Piccata

4 chicken cutlets
2 Tablespoons vegetable oil
1/4 cup dry white wine
1 teaspoon garlic, minced
1/2 cup chicken broth
2 Tablespoons fresh lemon juice
1 Tablespoon capers, drained
2 Tablespoons unsalted butter, melted
Lemon slices
Fresh parsley for garnishing

Season cutlets with salt and pepper and dust with flour. Coat sauté pan with nonstick spray, add oil, and heat over medium heat. Sauté cutlets 2 to 3 minutes, flip over, then sauté 1 to 2 minutes covered. Transfer cutlets to warm plate; pour fat from the pan. Deglaze pan with wine and add garlic. Cook until garlic is light brown, about 2 minutes. Add broth, lemon juice, and capers. Return cutlets to pan and cook 1 minute on each side. Transfer to a warm plate.

Sauce

Melt 2 tablespoons unsalted butter and add lemon slices. Pour over cutlets and garnish with parsley.

Anne Tenopir

Sunlight Chicken

8 chicken legs and thighs
1 teaspoon salt
1 teaspoon basil
1/2 teaspoon pepper
1/2 cup soy sauce
1/2 cup ketchup
1/4 cup honey
1/4 cup corn oil
2 cloves garlic, minced

Layer in a baking dish 8 chicken thighs and legs. Sprinkle with salt, basil, pepper. Pour over the chicken mixture of soy sauce, ketchup, honey, corn oil, and garlic. Bake at 350° for 1 hour or until juices run clear. Baste frequently. I like to serve this with a baked potato and a lettuce salad. Makes a wonderful meal anytime of the year.

Alice Dubs

I got this recipe from my best friend. I made it for Paul when we were engaged and working on digging a water line for the mobile home we were going to put on his Uncle Hank's place. Paul loved it, and it has been a favorite in our home ever since.

Grilled Chicken Cordon Bleu

4 boneless, skinless chicken breasts
8 slices thin Swiss cheese
8 slices thin deli ham
4 Tablespoons ranch dressing
Seasoning salt
2 Tablespoons olive oil
1/2 cup seasoned bread crumbs

Flatten the chicken to 1/4-inch thickness (pound between two pieces of plastic wrap). Spread 1 Tablespoon ranch dressing on each chicken breast; sprinkle with seasoning salt. Place 2 slices of cheese and 2 slices of ham on each to within 1/4 inch of the edge. Fold in thirds; secure with toothpicks. Roll in olive oil and then roll in bread crumbs. Grill covered over medium-hot heat for 15 minutes. Can assemble up to 8 hours in advance and keep in fridge. Makes 4 servings.

Carmelee Tuma, Assistant to Governor Dave Heineman

Oven-Baked Herb-Crusted Chicken

1 cup flour
2 teaspoons garlic powder
2 teaspoons onion powder
2 teaspoons mustard powder
2 teaspoons dried oregano
2 teaspoons dried thyme
2 teaspoons salt
1 teaspoon ground black pepper
12 (5-ounce) skinless, boneless chicken breast halves
Olive oil cooking spray

Preheat oven to 400°.

In 2 large zip-top bags, divide above ingredients into each bag. Place 6 chicken breasts in each bag. Seal the bags and shake to coat. Remove the chicken breasts, shaking off excess coating.

Transfer the chicken to a baking sheet and spray with olive oil cooking spray. Bake 15 to 30 minutes, until chicken is golden brown and cooked through.

Anita Wiechman

Wes Sheets grew up a farm boy in Kansas, became a fisheries biologist, and is now retired to the life of hunting and fishing to put meat on the table. This baked fish recipe came from one of the several trips between Alaska and the Gulf of Mexico. It is guaranteed to put pounds on your frame and really works with halibut or any other species.

Baked Halibut

2 pounds halibut fillets
1 pound butter, melted
1 pound Ritz crackers, crushed

Grease a 9 × 13-inch pan. Layer fish fillets in pan. Mix crushed crackers with melted butter and cover over halibut. Bake 400° for 20 minutes. Also great served with a cheese sauce.

Wes Sheets, Nebraska Game and Parks Commission

Fish in Salsa Sauce

1 pound tilapia fish (4 filets)
1 cup diced onion
1 clove garlic, chopped and diced
1/2 cup water
1 cup Pace salsa sauce
1 cup grated cheese

Sauté diced onion and garlic until translucent. Add salsa and water. Heat to combine. Lay the 4 filets in the pan and put the sauce on top. Let simmer until fish flakes easily. Add the grated cheese on top. Put the pan under the broiler until lightly brown. May serve with small red potatoes, vegetables, and a salad.

Kerstin O'Connor

Baked Stuffed Shrimp

18 large shrimp
1/2 cup salad oil
1/4 cup butter
1 clove garlic, crushed
1 1/2 teaspoons salt
1/2 teaspoon pepper

Stuffing

1 cup onion
1/2 cup bread crumbs
1 Tablespoon butter
2 Tablespoons sour cream
1 teaspoon salt
1/2 teaspoon thyme
1/2 teaspoon tarragon

Stuff shrimp. In a shallow baking dish, combine oil, butter, garlic, salt, and pepper. Heat in oven 5 minutes. Add stuffed shrimp. Cover with foil and bake at 350° for 15 to 20 minutes. Serves 6.

Anita Wiechman

Shrimp and Tortellini

1 pound unpeeled, medium-sized fresh shrimp
1 (9-ounce) package fresh or frozen tortellini with cheese filling,
**   uncooked**
1/3 cup butter or margarine
1 shallot, minced
1 Tablespoon chopped fresh basil or 2 teaspoons dried whole basil
1/2 cup grated Parmesan cheese

Peel and devein shrimp; set aside. Cook pasta according to the package directions; drain and set aside. Melt butter in large skillet over medium-high heat; add shrimp, minced shallot, and basil. Cook 5 minutes, stirring constantly. Add pasta and cheese. Toss gently, and garnish if desired. Best served immediately.

Great with a good salad and crusty bread. Serves 4, easily doubled.

Deb (Hohnstein) Schark

Seafood Strudel

1 small zucchini (about 8 ounces)
1 (10-ounce) package frozen chopped spinach, thawed and squeezed
    dry
1 (6 1/8- to 6 1/2-ounce) can tuna or salmon, packed in water, drained,
    or 1 pound mock crabmeat
1/2 (8-ounce) package light cream cheese, softened
3/4 cup part skim ricotta or cottage cheese
1/3 cup frozen no-cholesterol egg substitute, thawed, or 1 large egg
1/2 teaspoon salt
1/4 teaspoon dried dill weed
10 sheets fresh or frozen phyllo (about 1/3 of a 16-ounce package)
2 Tablespoons light corn-oil spread (1/4 stick), melted
1 Tablespoon seasoned dried bread crumbs

Coarsely shred zucchini. With paper towel, pat zucchini dry.

In bowl, mix zucchini with spinach, meat of your choice, cream cheese, ricotta cheese, egg substitute, salt, and dill weed.

Preheat oven to 375°. On waxed paper on work surface, place 2 sheets of phyllo, one on top of the other (each about 17 inches by 12 inches); brush very lightly with melted corn-oil spread; sprinkle with 1 teaspoon bread crumbs. Continue layering three more times; top with remaining 2 phyllo sheets.

Starting along the long side of phyllo, spoon the meat mixture to about 1/2 inch from edges to cover half of rectangle. From meat-mixture side, roll phyllo jelly-roll fashion.

Place roll, seam-side down, in jelly-roll pan. Brush with remaining melted

Meats, Poultry & Seafood

corn-oil spread. Cut 12 slashes on top of strudel. Bake 35 to 40 minutes until golden.

Cool strudel in pan on wire rack 5 minutes for easier slicing. Slice to serve.

Makes 6 main-dish servings.

Sheryl Thomsen

The needlepoint chairs in the lower level conference room at the Residence were created in 1986 through a statewide contest offered to all Nebraskans. Out of the ninety people who entered the contest, twenty-four ladies and one gentleman were selected to complete their designs. Each chair depicts a historic Nebraska building. On each chair is an abstract geological slice of the state: the underlying blue of the Ogallala aquifer, the brown of the soil, the green of the cornfields and the blue of the rivers, the gold of the wheatfields and grass-covered Sandhills, and a touch of red denoting the beautiful sunsets. Over all is the broad blue Nebraska sky.

The Lower Level Conference Room of the Residence is used for large group meetings and functions.

Meats, Poultry & Seafood

The original Formal Drawing Room.

Pies, Pastries & Desserts

The Formal Drawing Room

Much of the furniture in the Drawing Room is original to the Residence and has been refinished. The Formal Drawing Room has played host to numerous dignitaries over the years, including Bob Hope, actor Chuck Connors, and Senator John F. Kennedy.

The needlepoint chairs in the lower level conference room were created in 1986 through a statewide contest offered to all Nebraskans. Twenty-four ladies and one gentleman were selected to complete their design of a geographical slice of the state.

Pies, Pastries & Desserts

Amy's Cheesecake

Crust

1 cup graham cracker crumbs
3 Tablespoons sugar
3 Tablespoons melted butter or margarine

Combine crumbs, sugar, and butter; press into bottom of 9-inch spring-form pan. Bake at 325° for 10 minutes.

Filling

4 (8-ounce) packages of cream cheese, softened
1 cup sugar
3 Tablespoons flour
4 eggs
1 cup sour cream
1 Tablespoon real vanilla extract
1 (21-ounce) can cherry pie filling, or substitute any type of fresh fruit
   you prefer

Combine cream cheese, sugar, and flour, mixing at medium speed in electric mixer until well blended. Be sure to scrape down the sides of the bowl several times during this step. Add eggs, one at a time, mixing well after each addition. Again, it is important to scrape down the sides so there are not clumps of cream cheese in the batter. Blend in sour cream and vanilla.

Pour over crust. Bake at 450° for 10 minutes. Reduce oven temperature to 250° and continue baking 1 hour. Run knife around rim of pan to loosen cake. Cool before removing rim of pan. Chill.

My sister, Lorna, and I were very inventive in our playtime while living at the Governor's Residence. We had a "secret" hiding place in the basement under the steps. We would take our flashlights and cards and play Go Fish and Spoons for lengthy periods of time. We would hear our housekeeper, Marie De-Muth, calling our names, searching all over for us. We would giggle at the fact that she didn't know where we were. We never did give up our hiding place to her. We would also melt chocolate bars over the reading lamps in the living quarters so we could make s'mores without having to go downstairs to what we called the "big kitchen." And, of course, we would swim in the fountain in the backyard.

continued on page 214

Pies, Pastries & Desserts

continued from page 213

Unbeknownst to us the first time, there was blue dye in the fountain. Our mom was quite shocked to see us emerge with blue-tinted skin and our white blond hair not so white anymore. But it didn't stop us. Mom had to make sure we stayed out of the fountain if we had a formal function to attend. Then there was the time Chuck Connors, of The Rifleman, *was visiting. As the evening wore on, inhibitions were lost and he decided to slide down the banister. He lost his balance and, fortunately for him, fell toward the steps and not toward the marble floor below. He wore a large diamond ring that put a very large scratch in the blue flocked wallpaper. We have lots of fun memories like these from our days at the "Mansion."*

Top with fruit before serving, if desired. Also very good without fruit.

Amy Tieman Tipton

The Heritage Room in the lower level is used extensively for meetings, as well as for buffet setup for large functions. It houses the First Ladies' Doll Collection. The Distaff League of the Lutheran Medical Center in Omaha started the project in 1964, and the doll collection was put on permanent display in the Residence in 1974. Some of the Territorial Governor's wives were never included in the collection, and the Lincoln Doll Club is in the process of making those dolls so that the collection will be complete. First Gentleman Bill Orr has graciously consented to be shown in the collection.

Pies, Pastries & Desserts

Orange Almond Biscotti

4 cups flour
2 teaspoons baking powder
1/2 teaspoon salt
8 Tablespoons (1 stick) butter
2 cups sugar
4 large eggs
1 teaspoon vanilla extract
1/2 teaspoon almond extract
1 1/2 cups whole almonds with skins, toasted, then coarsely chopped
4 Tablespoons grated orange zest

Sift flour, baking powder, and salt together in a small bowl. Beat butter and sugar together until light and smooth. Add eggs, one at a time, then extracts. Stir in almonds and zest. Add dry ingredients until just mixed. Using floured hands, divide the dough into 4 equal parts. Form each part into a log (about 2 × 10 inches). Pat the logs into smoother oval logs. Wrap and refrigerate the logs for at least 2 hours on a cookie sheet; can go overnight. Place parchment paper on 2 cookie sheets. Unwrap and place 2 logs on each cookie sheet. Bake at 350° (325° in convection oven) for 20 to 30 minutes. Rotate the pans and exchange racks halfway through. Remove the biscotti with the parchment paper and cool for 10 minutes. Reduce oven temperature to 325° (300° in convection oven). Cut the biscotti into about 1-inch pieces on the diagonal and put back on the cookie sheet with new sheets of parchment paper. Bake for 15 minutes, turning the biscotti over at 7 minutes. Remove from oven and cool.

Biscotti must be completely cooled before storage to ensure that all the moisture has escaped.

In the Governor's Residence, there was always a cook to prepare the meals and a housekeeper to clean up, and we really weren't encouraged to be in the kitchen. There were four of us kids and my sisters were very young; we must have been too much for the kitchen staff. And since I was a teenager while Dad was in office, I was much too busy to cook, anyway. However, now my husband and I like nothing better than to have a glass of wine and cook together. He is an excellent cook and I have learned more about cooking from him than anyone else. Our children are great cooks as well, having been brought up sitting on the counter mixing ingredients or rolling dough, helping us prepare something delicious. My orange almond biscotti is one of our favorites.

Pies, Pastries & Desserts

To prevent the biscotti from becoming hard, put a slice of bread in the container with the biscotti. They will keep for at least 2 weeks, which is never a problem ... they won't last that long. Buon appetito!

Mary Tiemann DeLaney

The gowns worn by the Governor's wives in the First Ladies' Doll Collection have been reproduced as nearly as possible to duplicate the original ball gowns or, in some cases, dresses of the period. Many of the First Ladies have donated memorabilia for the exhibit.

Pies, Pastries & Desserts

Gene Autry's Peanut Butter Pie

1 cup peanut butter
1 (8-ounce) package cream cheese
1 cup sugar
2 Tablespoons melted butter
1 cup whipping cream
1 Tablespoon vanilla
1 graham cracker pie crust
Hot fudge sauce

Cream together peanut butter, cream cheese, and sugar. Stir in butter, whipping cream, and vanilla. Mix well. Pour into pie crust and chill 4 to 5 hours until set. Top with thinned hot fudge sauce. Chill again for 30 minutes.

Staci Hawley

This pie is absolutely wonderful. It's a "Girls' Pie and Coffee Day" favorite.

Pies, Pastries & Desserts

My mother, Iva Anderson, owned and operated the Hilltop Café in Oakland, Nebraska, for almost twenty-five years. Every day she made three to five homemade pies using this crust recipe. She was known for her great pies.

'Hilltop Café' Pie Crust

4 1/2 cups flour
1 teaspoon salt
1 teaspoon baking powder
1 Tablespoon sugar
1 pound lard
1/2 cup water
1 teaspoon vinegar
1 egg

Sift the dry ingredients together. Blend the lard into the dry-ingredient mixture. Combine water, vinegar, and egg, and beat. Add to flour mixture and blend well. Form 8 balls. Store in Ziploc bags and refrigerate or freeze. They will keep a long time if frozen.

Nancy Enstrom

Pies, Pastries & Desserts

Mabel's Shoofly Pie

9-inch pastry shell
1/3 cup melted butter
2/3 cup sugar
2/3 cup dark corn syrup
2/3 cup regular oatmeal (not quick)
3 beaten eggs
1/2 teaspoon salt
1 teaspoon vanilla
1/2 cup coconut
1 cup coarsely chopped pecans

In 2-quart mixing bowl, stir all filling ingredients together and pour into prepared pie shell. Bake at 350° for 40 to 45 minutes, until filling is set in center.

Serves 8.

Ninajean Bryan Rohlfs

My great-grandmother, Mabel Jones Bryan, who was born in Tennessee, was an amazing woman. This is great-grandma's recipe for a Southern specialty she made that proved to be cousin William Jennings Bryan's favorite dessert. It's a heritage food I enjoy making for Bryan holiday gatherings a century later!

Pies, Pastries & Desserts

Mom's Favorite Sour Cream Raisin Pie

This is a very rich dessert ... a family favorite, made for special holidays and celebrations.

1 (9-inch) pie shell (baked)
1 1/4 cups sugar
1 1/2 Tablespoons flour
1 1/2 cups sour cream
3 egg yolks
1 1/2 teaspoons cinnamon
1 1/2 cups cooked raisins (drained)
1 1/2 Tablespoons vinegar
1 1/2 teaspoons vanilla

Stir sugar and flour together. Beat egg yolks slightly. Mix sugar, flour, egg yolks, sour cream, cinnamon, and raisins together. Cook until thick. I do this in the microwave on medium power. Stir in vinegar and vanilla. Pour into a baked 9-inch pie shell. Top with meringue made with the 3 egg whites and bake until the meringue is brown.

Senator Gail and Mary Lou Kopplin

Pies, Pastries & Desserts

Pineapple-Rhubarb Pie

Crust

9-inch double crust

Filling

1 (8 3/4-ounce) can crushed pineapple, not drained
4 cups diced rhubarb
1 1/2 cups sugar
3/4 cup flour
1/4 teaspoon pineapple flavoring
1/4 teaspoon lemon flavoring

Mix together and spoon into pastry-lined pie pan. Dot with 2 Tablespoons butter. Cover with top crust. Let stand for 20 minutes. Bake at 400° for 40 minutes.

Senator Deb Fischer

There are great cooks in the 43rd District and good pies are a community tradition for carry-in dinners. This is one of my favorites, although my husband, Bruce, and our three sons' favorite is my peach pie!

Pies, Pastries & Desserts

District 22 has a rich heritage of German, Polish, and Czech nationalities, from which many good cooks come. This pie is a favorite for the countless church dinners, fundraisers, county fairs, and plain-old family get-togethers. I love to bake for the enjoyment of my family and friends.

Plain-Jane Apple Pie

Crust

9-inch double crust

Filling

6 cups peeled, sliced tart green cooking apples (about 2 pounds or 6 medium)
1 cup granulated sugar
1/3 cup firmly packed brown sugar
3 Tablespoons all-purpose flour
1 teaspoon cinnamon
3 Tablespoons butter or margarine, softened

For filling, combine apples, granulated sugar, brown sugar, flour, cinnamon, and butter in a large bowl. Toss to coat. Spoon into unbaked crust. Moisten pastry edge with water. Roll top crust same as bottom. Lift onto pie. Trim 1/2 inch beyond edge of pie plate. Fold top edge under bottom crust and flute. Bake at 425° for 10 minutes. Reduce oven temperature to 325°. Cover edge with foil, if necessary, to prevent overbrowning. Bake 40 minutes or until filling center is bubbly and crust is golden brown. Cool to room temperature before serving.

Senator Arnie and Nancy Stuthman

Pies, Pastries & Desserts

Reka's Mincemeat Pie

3 pounds beef neck meat, boiled and ground (I now use a 2- to 3-pound beef roast)
1 quart meat juice
10 pounds sour apples, ground
1 1/2 pounds suet (I now use 1 cup canola oil)
2 pounds seedless raisins
2 pounds currants
4 pounds brown sugar
3 large Tablespoons salt
2 cups apple-cider vinegar
3 pints corn syrup
3 teaspoons nutmeg
3 teaspoons ground cloves
1/4 cup cinnamon
1 pint apple juice or brandy

Bring all ingredients to a good boil. Cool and pack to freeze. You can cut the recipe in half and still have plenty of mincemeat for holiday sharing.

Lee Rockwell

I was raised with this version of mincemeat pie and thought that all mincemeat was the same. Wrong! This mincemeat that is a family tradition was named in honor of my grandmother, Reka Stading Rahn Ehmke, who immigrated to this country in 1868 from a small village in the lowlands of Germany. The apple juice version was served to friends in the community, then for family gatherings the pint of whiskey was pulled out from its hiding place and the mincemeat was laced with it prior to baking. Ah! What an aroma!

Pies, Pastries & Desserts

My mother used to serve our family rhubarb pie made from rhubarb grown on our farm. I added the strawberries to rhubarb grown on my husband's and my farm to serve to my own family. It is the most requested recipe when everyone returns for a visit.

Strawberry-Rhubarb Pie

Pastry for two-crust pie
1 1/4 cups sugar
1/8 teaspoon salt
1/3 cup flour
2 cups fresh strawberries
2 cups (1-inch pieces) fresh rhubarb
2 Tablespoons butter or margarine
1 Tablespoon sugar

Mix sugar mixture with the strawberries and rhubarb. Arrange in pastry-lined 9-inch pie pan. Dot with butter. Place top crust on pan and flute edges. Brush top of pie with cold water and sprinkle on 1 Tablespoon sugar. Cut steam vents. Bake in hot (425°) oven for 40 to 50 minutes.

Jan Hibbs

Pies, Pastries & Desserts

Watermelon Pie

1 (9-inch) prepared graham cracker crust
1 (3-ounce) package watermelon-flavored gelatin
1/4 cup water
1 (12-ounce) container frozen whipped topping, thawed
2 cups watermelon chunks or balls (seeds removed)

Mix together the watermelon gelatin and water. Fold gelatin mixture into the dessert topping and add cut watermelon. Pour mixture into graham cracker crust. Cool in refrigerator for about 3 hours.

Senator Mike and Mandi Flood

Madison County is known for great watermelons—the sandy riverbottom soil is ideal for growing them.

The Heritage Room contains the beginnings of a library of books by Nebraska authors. Many of the books are autographed. The Nebraska Library Commission is working on expanding the collection.

Pies, Pastries & Desserts

Jennifer Pansing makes a similar crisp, using tart cherries. She was happy to learn that Nebraska City grows wonderful cherries as well as their famous apples.

Extra-Special Apple Crisp

6 cups or more sliced apples
1 cup sugar
1 cup water
2 Tablespoons cornstarch
1 teaspoon cinnamon

Topping

1 cup flour
3/4 cup quick oatmeal
1 cup brown sugar
1/2 cup butter, melted

Put apples in a 9 × 13-inch or 11 × 13-inch pan. Boil sugar, water, and cornstarch together over low heat until thick and clear. Pour over apples. Combine remaining ingredients, sprinkle over apples, and bake at 350° for 40 minutes or until apples are done. Note: This is very good using 2/3 apples and 1/3 peaches for fruit. Fresh peaches or well-drained canned peaches may be used.

Senator Arnie and Nancy Stuthman

Pies, Pastries & Desserts

My Apple Cobbler

8 to 10 peeled and sliced Nebraska City apples
2 cups sugar
3 teaspoons cinnamon
Dash of salt
7 Tablespoons flour
1 teaspoon nutmeg
1/2 cup water

Topping

2 cups flour
1 cup margarine, melted
1 1/3 cups sugar
1 cup pecans

Butter a 9 × 13-inch cake pan. Slice Nebraska City-grown apples into cake pan. Mix sugar, cinnamon, salt, flour, and nutmeg and spread over apples. Pour water over mixture in pan. Mix flour, melted margarine, and sugar, then drop mixture over the apples. Sprinkle pecans on top. Bake approximately 50 minutes at 350° or until golden brown.

Deb Fox

This was my mother's recipe and is a favorite of our family. This recipe was a prize winner in the Nebraska City AppleJack Festival Recipe Contest.

Pies, Pastries & Desserts

In the late summer of 1865, three scouts were sent from a German Lutheran settlement near Ixonia, Wisconsin, near Waterton to find productive, inexpensive farmland. They traveled from Chicago to St. Joseph, Missouri, by train, then took a ferry to Omaha. Along their travels, they stopped by what is now West Point, but due to overpopulation they continued on and settled in Madison County. A year later, forty-two families set out in three wagon trains and settled the area of what is now Norfolk, Nebraska. They brought with them a love of German cooking that is still evident in the Norfolk area.

Apple Strudel

1 pound sweet apples, peeled, cored, and thinly sliced
1/4 cup golden raisins
1/4 cup dried currants
1/2 teaspoon ground cinnamon
2 Tablespoons white sugar
2 slices brown bread, crumbled
1/2 (16-ounce) package phyllo dough
1/4 cup butter, melted

Preheat oven to 400°. Combine apples, raisins, currants, cinnamon, sugar, and bread crumbs. Stir well. Spread sheets of phyllo generously with melted butter and lay them one atop the other on a baking sheet. Spread the fruit mixture evenly over the top sheet, then roll the sheets up to form a log shape. Brush with melted butter again. Bake in preheated oven for 30 minutes until the pastry is golden brown and the fruit is tender.

Senator Mike and Mandi Flood

Pies, Pastries & Desserts

Peach Cobbler

This is a simple cobbler that I often take to county gatherings.

4 cups peaches
1/4 cup orange or pineapple juice
1 cup self-rising flour
1 cup sugar
1 cup milk
1 stick butter
Nutmeg and cinnamon, to taste

Peel and slice peaches. Pour juice and a little sugar over the slices. Sprinkle with nutmeg and cinnamon. Mix flour, sugar, and milk to make topping. Melt butter in a 9 × 13-inch pan. Pour in fruit mixture, top with topping mixture, and bake 45 minutes at 350°.

Senator Vickie McDonald

Pies, Pastries & Desserts

Gladys often shared these tea logs at Maria Lutheran Church and Hershey fundraisers. They always sold out very early.

Swedish Tea Logs

1/4 cup warm water
1 package dry yeast
2 cups flour
2 Tablespoons sugar
1/2 teaspoon salt
1/4 teaspoon baking soda
1/2 cup soft butter
1/2 cup currants
1/4 cup evaporated milk
1/4 cup water
1 beaten egg yolk

Combine yeast and water. Stir together dry ingredients, cut in butter. Combine dry ingredients, yeast, currants, evaporated milk, water, and beaten egg yolk. Mix well. Chill dough 2 hours or overnight.

Filling

1/2 cup chopped pecans
1/4 cup melted butter
1/2 cup brown sugar

Divide dough in half. Roll each half into a 6 × 18-inch rectangle. Combine melted butter, brown sugar, and chopped pecan; spread over dough. Roll up as for jelly-roll. Cut into thirds. Snip and twist as in making a tea ring, but do not make a circle. Let rise 30 minutes. Bake at 400° for 20 minutes.

Pies, Pastries & Desserts

Frosting

2 Tablespoons butter, browned
1 cup powdered sugar
1/2 teaspoon vanilla

Stir together browned butter, powdered sugar, and vanilla. Add enough evaporated milk to make a frosting of desired consistency. Spread or drizzle over tea log. May decorate with candied cherries and pineapple.

Gladys Jorgenson

In 1947, MGM made a film on the McKelvie Ranch located in the Sandhills of Nebraska. Shortly after, former Governor Sam McKelvie commissioned the painting Sea of Grass, found in the Heritage Room. The painting was presented to Governor Jim Exon in 1976 by Mr. K. M. Brown, nephew of Governor McKelvie.

Pies, Pastries & Desserts

What family doesn't have a sweet tooth for chocolate, and what family doesn't have a few nuts in it? This recipe combines both of these ingredients in a sweet and tasty treat. The "mud" is the chocolate, of course. With white chocolate, dark chocolate, peanut butter, and cashews, what's not to love? It's fast and easy to make.

Peanut Butter Mud Bars

8 Tablespoons (1 stick or 1/2 cup) unsalted butter, softened
1 cup firmly packed light brown sugar
1/2 cup creamy peanut butter
2 large eggs, at room temperature
1 Tablespoon pure vanilla extract
1 cup all-purpose flour
1 teaspoon baking soda
1/4 teaspoon salt
4 ounces white chocolate chips
4 ounces semisweet chocolate chips
1/2 cup chopped cashews

Topping

4 ounces white chocolate chips
4 ounces semisweet chocolate chips
1/2 cup chopped cashews

Preheat oven to 350°. Line a 9 × 12-inch baking pan with nonstick foil. In a large bowl, cream butter and brown sugar until smooth. Add peanut butter and mix on medium speed; add eggs and vanilla extract, mixing to combine. In medium bowl, whisk together flour, baking soda, and salt. Add flour mixture, stirring to combine. Fold in white chocolate chips, semisweet chocolate chips, and chopped cashews. Spread batter evenly in pan. Bake 30 minutes or until center tests done. Do not overbake or bars will be crumbly. Immediately upon removing bars from the oven, sprinkle remaining white and semisweet chocolate chips on hot bars. Cover loosely with foil and set aside for about 5 minutes until chocolates are soft. Use a toothpick to create a

Pies, Pastries & Desserts

swirled, marbleized effect in the soft chocolate. Sprinkle with remaining 1/2 cup cashews. Let bars cool before cutting into 24 to 48 cookies.

Kathy Baugh

A model of the USS Nebraska, commissioned in 1993, is displayed in the Heritage Room. The model was given to Nebraska by the men and women of Electric Boat Co. of Groton, Connecticut. The Ohio Class Trident nuclear submarine, nicknamed "Big Red," is as long as a fifty-six-story building.

Pies, Pastries & Desserts

I inherited my mom's copy of this recipe that is a small scrap of paper cut from Kitchen Klatter Magazine *back in the 1960s. My mother listened to Leanna Driftmeier and eventually Leanna's daughters, Lucile and Marjery, on the radio every weekday. They had a half-hour program called "Kitchen Klatter" and also a magazine by the same name with stories and recipes. Every day when the program was over, there would be scribbling of recipes on any scrap of paper that my mom could find handy. There weren't always titles for those recipes, but she knew what they were supposed to be. The important ingredients that make these bars so good are the real butter and what used to be called "Kitchen Klatter Lemon Flavoring."*

Prize-Winning Lemon Squares

2 cups flour
1/2 cup powdered sugar
1 cup butter or margarine
2 cups sugar
1/2 teaspoon salt
4 Tablespoons flour
1 teaspoon baking powder
4 eggs, lightly beaten
4 Tablespoons lemon juice
1/2 teaspoon Kitchen Klatter Lemon Flavoring

Mix flour, powdered sugar, and butter and press into a 9 × 13-inch pan. Bake 20 minutes at 350°. Sift sugar, salt, flour, and baking powder. Beat eggs until light. Stir in sifted dry ingredients and lemon juice and flavoring. Pour over baked hot crust layer. Return to oven for 25 minutes. Cut into squares while warm. Sift powdered sugar over the top before removing from the pan.

Cindy Stolberg

Pies, Pastries & Desserts

Treasure Bars

1 cup flour
1/2 cup brown sugar
1/2 cup butter

Combine flour and brown sugar; cut in butter. Press into a 9 × 13-inch pan and bake 10 minutes at 350°.

Topping

1 cup brown sugar
2 slightly beaten eggs
1 Tablespoon flour
1/2 teaspoon baking powder
1/4 teaspoon salt
1 cup shredded coconut
1/2 to 3/4 cup chocolate chips
Nuts (optional)

Gradually add 1 cup brown sugar to eggs, beating until light and fluffy. Add dry ingredients; stir in coconut and chocolate chips. Spread over baked crust and bake about 20 minutes or until top is nicely browned.

Diane Rogert, mother of Senator Kent Rogert

This recipe is from Elva Hansen, Senator Kent Rogert's grandmother. It has been a family favorite (and Kent's) for years. I have taken these bars to many events and have always been asked for the recipe. Even people who don't think they like coconut like these bars.

Pies, Pastries & Desserts

This is long-time family-favorite recipe. Even people who think they don't like rhubarb seem to enjoy it.

Rhubarb Bars

Rhubarb Mixture

3 cups rhubarb cut into 1-inch pieces (6 or 7 big stalks)
1 1/2 cups sugar
3 Tablespoons cornstarch dissolved in 1/2 cup water
1 teaspoon vanilla

Mix together and heat to a boil (9 to 10 minutes in the microwave). Then set aside to cool.

Crust

1 1/2 cups oatmeal
1 1/2 cups flour
1 cup brown sugar
1/2 teaspoon baking soda
1 cup margarine, melted
1/2 cup chopped nuts (optional)

Mix well and pat 3/4 of mixture in bottom of a 9 × 13-inch pan. Spread with rhubarb mixture and top with rest of crumb mixture. Bake at 350° for 30 to 35 minutes.

Senator John and Janet Wightman

Pies, Pastries & Desserts

Danish Apple Bars

My family has always loved this dessert.

2 1/2 cups flour
1 teaspoon salt
1 cup shortening
1 egg yolk and milk to make 2/3 cup
4 large apples (4 cups peeled and sliced)
1 cup crushed cornflakes
1 teaspoon cinnamon, or more to taste
1 cup sugar
1 beaten egg white
1 cup powdered sugar
1 teaspoon water
1 teaspoon vanilla

Cut shortening into flour and salt; add milk (with egg yolk). Roll out 1/2 of dough, put in greased 15 1/2 × 10 1/2-inch pan. Place apples over dough. Sprinkle with cornflakes, cinnamon, and sugar. Roll out remainder of dough and put on top. Brush with beaten egg white and sprinkle with sugar. Bake at 375° for 1 hour. Glaze while warm with a mixture of powdered sugar, water, and vanilla.

Senator Vickie McDonald

Pies, Pastries & Desserts

This recipe was given to me by a friend who lives on the edge of the beautiful Niobrara River. She is famous for always having something good to eat at her house. I now use it for special times when family and friends drop in.

Easy Brownies ... To Knock Your Socks Off!

2 sticks butter or margarine, melted
2 cups sugar
4 eggs
1 teaspoon vanilla
1/4 cup cocoa
1 1/2 cups flour
1/4 cup white baking chips
1/4 cup milk chocolate chips
1/4 cup chopped walnuts or pecans

Melt butter or margarine over medium heat; add 2 cups sugar, mix well, and let cool slightly. Beat eggs and add to the butter-sugar mixture along with the vanilla, cocoa, and flour. Beat well and pour into well-greased 9 × 13-inch pan. Sprinkle with chips and nuts, but do not mix into batter. Bake at 350° for about 35 minutes. Cool slightly before cutting into squares, if you can wait that long.

Gwen Johnson Otto, Regent, Lone Willow DAR

Pies, Pastries & Desserts

Scandinavian Almond Bars

1 3/4 cups all-purpose flour
2 teaspoons baking powder
1/4 teaspoon salt
1 cup sugar
1/2 cup butter or margarine
1 egg
1/2 teaspoon almond extract
Milk
1/2 cup sliced almonds, coarsely chopped

Almond Icing

1 cup sifted powdered sugar
1/4 teaspoon almond extract
Milk

Stir together flour, baking powder, and salt. Mix sugar and butter in separate bowl. Beat until fluffy. Add egg and almond extract and beat well. Add flour mixture and beat until well mixed.

Divide dough into fourths. Form each into a 12-inch roll. Place 2 rolls 4 to 5 inches apart on an ungreased cookie sheet. Flatten with your fingers until it is 3 inches wide. Repeat with the other rolls.

Brush flattened rolls with milk and sprinkle with almonds. Bake at 325° for 12 to 14 minutes, or until edges are lightly browned. While cookies are still warm, cut them crosswise at a diagonal into 1-inch strips. Cool. Drizzle with almond icing.

Pies, Pastries & Desserts

Makes 48 bars.

For almond icing, stir together sifted powdered sugar, almond extract, and enough milk (3 to 4 teaspoons) to make icing that is of drizzling consistency.

Sheila Swanson

The portrait at the foot of the stairway in the lower level is of General "Black Jack" Pershing; it was painted by Mrs. Martha McKelvie, First Lady of Nebraska from 1919–1923.

Pies, Pastries & Desserts

Chocolate Franges

1 box vanilla wafers
1 cup butter
2 cups sifted powdered sugar
4 squares bitter chocolate, melted
2 teaspoons vanilla
4 eggs
Optional: 1 teaspoon peppermint flavoring

Beat together the butter and powdered sugar; add melted chocolate, vanilla, and eggs. Beat well. Line small cups or glasses with crushed vanilla wafers, fill with chocolate mixture, and sprinkle with more vanilla wafer crumbs. Freeze.

Former First Lady Ruth Thone

We call these "the chocolate things," and since they are frozen, they're really good for those times when you're hungry for you-don't-know-what and are delighted to discover there are "chocolate things" in the freezer!

Pies, Pastries & Desserts

This was the Grand Prize Winner in the First Annual Nebraska City AppleJack Recipe Contest. The judges graded on a scale of one to five on appearance, texture, quantity of locally grown apples, uniqueness, ease of preparation, and taste. We encourage people to come to Nebraska City to visit our orchards and enjoy the locally grown apples.

Caramel Apple Cheesecake

Crust

1/2 cup butter, softened
1/2 cup packed brown sugar
2 cups flour
1/2 cup quick oatmeal
1/2 cup finely chopped pecans
1 teaspoon ground cinnamon

Filling

3 (8-ounce) packages cream cheese, softened
1 can (14-ounce) sweetened condensed milk
1/4 to 1 teaspoon ground cinnamon, to taste
1/2 cup apple juice concentrate
3 eggs, slightly beaten

Topping

2 to 3 medium Nebraska City apples, peeled and sliced
1 Tablespoon butter
1 teaspoon cornstarch
1/4 to 1/2 teaspoon ground cinnamon
1/4 cup apple juice concentrate
1/4 cup brown sugar

Optional: Caramel apple dip (drizzle)

Preheat oven to 325° and place 9 × 13-inch pan of water on the lower shelf of

Pies, Pastries & Desserts

the oven. Cut an 11-inch circle of parchment paper and place in the bottom of a 9-inch spring-form pan. In a small mixing bowl, cream butter and brown sugar. Gradually add flour, oats, pecans, and cinnamon; mix well. Press onto bottom and up sides of spring-form pan. Bake for 10 minutes or until set. Cool on wire rack. Swirl warmed caramel apple dip over crust. In a large mixing bowl, beat cream cheese until fluffy. Beat in condensed milk, apple juice concentrate, and cinnamon until smooth. Add eggs and beat on low speed until just combined (batter will be thin). Pour over crust and caramel dip. Bake at 325° for 40 to 45 minutes or until center is almost set. Cool on wire rack for 10 minutes. Carefully run knife around edge of pan to loosen; cool 1 hour longer. Refrigerate overnight.

Remove cheesecake from pan. In a large skillet, cook and stir apples in butter, brown sugar, and cinnamon over medium heat until crisp-tender (about 5 minutes). Cool to room temperature. Arrange apples over cheesecake. In a small saucepan, combine cornstarch, apple juice concentrate, and cinnamon until smooth. Bring to a boil, stirring constantly. Boil for 1 minute or until cinnamon is smooth. Bring to a boil, stirring constantly. Boil for 1 minute or until thickened. Immediately brush over apples. Refrigerate for 1 hour or until chilled.

Rhonda Nielson

Pies, Pastries & Desserts

This ice cream will keep in the deep freeze for several months. This recipe was given to us by my mother and has been used on a number of occasions when we have entertained senators at our home. We always have lots of toppings available.

Herb's Vanilla Ice Cream

5 large or 6 small eggs (we recommend a pasteurized egg product)
1/4 teaspoon salt
2 1/8 cups sugar
2 Tablespoons vanilla
1 pint heavy cream

Mix together and pour into ice cream freezer and fill with milk until about three-quarters full. Freeze.

Senator DiAnna Schimek

Someone always asks for the recipe when I take this dessert somewhere.

Ice Cream Sandwich Dessert

2 packages of 12 ice cream sandwiches (24 total)
1 large container Cool Whip
1 large jar hot fudge ice cream topping
1 can salted peanuts

Line a 9 × 13-inch pan with ice cream sandwiches, cut to fit. Spread 1/2 jar hot fudge topping over the sandwiches. Spread 1/2 Cool Whip over the hot fudge. Sprinkle with peanuts. Add another layer of ice cream sandwiches, hot fudge topping, and Cool Whip, and sprinkle with peanuts. Freeze. You will have a few ice cream sandwiches left over. I sometimes use praline crunch between the layers and peanuts on top.

Carol A. Lewis

Pies, Pastries & Desserts

Mexican Fried Ice Cream (Without Frying)

1 gallon ice cream (or more depending on the number of people being served)
1 to 2 cups crushed corn flakes
Honey
Cinnamon

Using an ice cream scoop, make solid balls of ice cream. Roll balls in honey and then in crushed corn flakes. At this point, you can drizzle more honey on top of the ice cream balls and sprinkle with cinnamon. Freeze until ready to eat.

Mary Catherine Rodriquez

Listy (Leaves)

3 large eggs, beaten
1 Tablespoon sugar
1 Tablespoon milk
2 cups (approximately) all-purpose flour

Mix eggs, sugar, and milk together. Add enough flour to make the dough the consistency of pie crust. Roll out the dough on lightly floured surface as thin as pie dough. Cut into 2 × 2-inch squares. Prick each piece with a fork several times. Fry in 1-inch of oil at 375° until golden brown. Put on paper towel and sprinkle with granulated sugar or powdered sugar.

Norma J. Most Kotas

This recipe was handed down to me by my mother-in-law, Bessie Masek Kotas, who came to Nebraska from Hriskove, Czechoslovakia, in 1913 at the age of sixteen. The original recipe from Czechoslovakia used cream and the dough was fried in lard.

Pies, Pastries & Desserts

This has become a holiday favorite for our family. It started with Grannie Kottas making it for every family get-together. As she got older and it became more difficult for her to cook, it was passed on to me, and now I am the one who brings it to every family event. It is so easy to make that now our kids almost do it all by themselves, while Russ and I look on and offer guidance if needed.

Cranberry Dessert

1 pound cranberries, ground
1 cup sugar
1 pint whipping cream, lightly whipped
3/4 pound small marshmallows
1 cup drained pineapple tidbits
3/4 cup chopped nuts

Mix ground cranberries and 1 cup sugar together and let stand for 2 hours in the refrigerator. In another bowl, mix whipped cream and marshmallows and refrigerate for 2 hours. Mix the two together, adding pineapple and nuts. Let stand overnight.

Senator Russ and Jill Karpisek

Lieutenant John J. Pershing came to the University of Nebraska as a military commander in 1891 and helped to change the destiny of the Nebraska band. Before he came on the scene, the band stood in formation and played while the cadets marched. Pershing, however, required the band to march as well as play during military drill. The cadets and band won several honors for their precision and began to draw large crowds at their weekly reviews. Pershing was a sports fan, and he suggested that the cadets and band put on a review during a football game. This first "halftime show" was performed in November 1893 and became an annual event.

Pies, Pastries & Desserts

Chocolate Bread Pudding

8 slices dry bread, cubed (4 cups)
4 Tablespoons cocoa powder
4 cups milk
6 egg yolks (save whites for making the meringue)
1 Tablespoon sugar
1 cup sugar

Meringue

6 egg whites
1/2 teaspoon cream of tartar
1 teaspoon vanilla
3/4 cups sugar

Butter 9 × 13-inch cake pan. Place bread cubes in a 2-quart saucepan. Sprinkle the 4 Tablespoons cocoa powder over the bread cubes. Pour 4 cups milk over all and heat until just scalded, stirring continuously. Add 1 Tablespoon sugar to the scalded-milk mixture. Beat egg yolks, mix with 1 cup sugar, and add to the scalded mixture. Pour into prepared pan. Bake at 350° for 30 minutes until set.

Top with meringue. It is best to make the meringue during the last 10 minutes of pudding-baking time. Beat the 6 egg whites with 1/4 teaspoon cream of tartar and 1 teaspoon vanilla until soft peaks form. Gradually add 3/4 cup sugar and keep beating until meringue holds stiff peaks. Bake at 350° 12 to 15 minutes until peaks of meringue are golden.

Gloria Kriete

My grandmother, Nellie Badgley, was born in Butler County in 1891. This is a recipe that Nellie got from her mother and handed down to my mother. Nellie added the meringue to the dessert instead of using the whole egg in the pudding. Even though I don't have an abundance of eggs from my own chickens, I do save the heels of bread and make this dessert when I want something easy that looks like a fancy dessert. Many people don't realize it is a bread pudding.

Grandma Hannah brought this bread pudding recipe with her to America from Skane, Sweden. This is an easy recipe, and it is good.

Grandma Hannah's Bread Pudding

4 cups milk
2 cups coffee bread
2 eggs, slightly beaten
1/2 teaspoon salt
3/4 cup sugar
1/2 teaspoon vanilla
3 Tablespoons melted butter

Scald milk and mash coffee bread into it; add eggs, salt, sugar, and vanilla. Over this, pour melted butter. Bake in pan or casserole for at least 1 hour at 300°. Take from oven and spread grape jelly over top. Beat 2 egg whites until stiff but not dry. Gradually beat in 4 Tablespoons sugar. Pile on top of jelly and put bread pudding back in oven until meringue is lightly browned.

Wanda Lambourn

Pies, Pastries & Desserts

Cottage Cheese Varenikje

Dough Mixture

2 1/2 cups sifted all-purpose flour
1 teaspoon salt
3 egg whites
1/2 cup milk
1/2 cup half-and-half

Cottage Cheese Filling

2 1/2 cups dry or baker's cottage cheese
3 egg yolks
1/2 teaspoon salt
Dash of cinnamon
1 teaspoon minced onion

Combine flour and salt in a deep bowl. Make a well in the center. Add egg whites and liquids; knead together. Turn out onto a floured board and knead until dough is smooth. Too much kneading can toughen dough. Divide into 2 parts. Cover and let stand in refrigerator all morning or all day.

Prepare cottage cheese filling by mixing all ingredients. Set aside. Roll dough very thin on lightly floured board. Cut rounds with a 3-inch biscuit cutter or with open end of a glass. Place a spoonful of filling in the center. Moisten edges with water or use a little flour and pinch edges together to make a secure seal. Drop a few varenikje at a time into a large kettle of rapidly boiling salted water. Do not cook too many at a time. Stir gently with a wooden spoon to separate them and prevent them from sticking to the bottom of the pot. Continue boiling for 3 to 4 minutes. Varenikje are ready when they are

Varenyky, from the Russian, are small dough pockets that are filled with cottage cheese. Varenikje is the Mennonite derivation of the word. Varenyky is a favorite national dish of the Ukraine. Brought by Tartars from the east, dumplings gradually became a permanent part of the Russian cuisine. Fillings vary, but the most popular is cottage cheese. In the summer, dumplings may be filled with fruit: cherries, apricots, berries, or plums. The finishing touch is a sprinkling of sugar and a dollop of sour cream or a sweet cream-and-butter sauce.

Pies, Pastries & Desserts

well puffed. Remove with perforated spoon to a colander and drain thoroughly. You may dribble a little melted butter or margarine between the varenikje to keep them from sticking. At this point, some families prefer their varenikje browned in butter in a hot skillet. Serve hot with either cream gravy or syrup. Leftover varenikje may be cut in strips, reheated, and served the next day.

Cream Gravy

2 to 3 Tablespoons butter
1 cup heavy sour cream

Combine butter and sour cream. Warm over medium heat.

Fried Molasses Syrup

1/2 cup molasses
Sugar, to taste
Water to thin slightly

Heat the molasses in the same heavy skillet in which the varenikje is fried. Add a little water and sugar, bringing mixture to a boil. Serve over varenikje and top with sour cream.

Jean Peters

Harriet's Swedish Rice Pudding

1 1/2 cups cooked white rice (not instant)
4 eggs
1/2 cup sugar
3 cups milk
Dash of salt
1 teaspoon vanilla

Beat the eggs slightly, by hand and add the sugar and mix well. Add the milk, salt, vanilla, and rice. Mix and place in a 2-quart buttered casserole. Set casserole dish in a 9 × 13-inch pan that contains about 1/2 inch of water. Stir mixture one more time. Bake at 325° for 1 1/2 hours. The rice pudding is done when a small knife inserted in the center comes out clean.

Serves 6.

Senator Tom and Margo Carlson

Tom's mother was a wonderful woman, gifted in the art of hospitality, so that everyone who knew her loved her. Invited guests as well as those who stopped in unexpectedly were all treated to something good to eat and a great cup of coffee. Tom's heritage is 100 percent Swedish, and this recipe for rice pudding was passed down as a family favorite.

This recipe is one that my grandfather, Jurgen Henry Andresen, brought with him from Denmark when he came to America in 1868. He and his wife celebrated their sixtieth wedding anniversary in 1935, which was almost unheard of in those days.

Maybiddle Pudding

Pudding

1 cup sugar
1/2 cup butter
1 teaspoon salt
2 1/2 teaspoons baking powder
2 whole eggs
1 cup whole milk
2 1/2 cups raisins
Flour to make a stiff dough

Steam over hot water for 3 hours or until set. Serve with lemon sauce.

Lemon Sauce

1 cup sugar
2 Tablespoons flour
1/4 teaspoon salt
1 cup whole milk
2 eggs, separated
1 large lemon

Remove rind from lemon with a fine grater. Mix milk, well-beaten egg yolks, salt, juice from lemon, and grated rind. Cook over medium heat, stirring constantly until thick and creamy. Fold in stiffly beaten egg whites. Serve warm over Maybiddle Pudding.

Moniema Andresen Niemeyer

Christmas Plum Pudding

1/2 cup apple, chopped
1/2 cup suet, chopped
1/2 cup molasses
2 eggs, well beaten
1/2 cup milk
2 cups sifted flour
1/4 cup figs, chopped
1/2 cup raisins
1/2 cup currants
1/4 cup citron, sliced
1/4 cup candied cherries, quartered
1 Tablespoon candied orange peel, chopped
1/4 cup almonds, blanched and chopped
2 teaspoons Calumet Baking Powder
1/2 teaspoon salt
1/2 teaspoon soda
1/2 teaspoon cinnamon
1/4 teaspoon allspice
1/2 teaspoon nutmeg

Combine apple, suet, molasses, eggs, and milk. Sift flour once, measure. Mix 1/2 cup flour with fruit and nuts. Combine remaining flour, baking powder, salt, soda, and spices, then sift again. Add to molasses mixture and add fruit. Turn into well-greased molds, filling them 2/3 full. Cover tightly and steam for 3 hours. Serve hot with hard sauce.

Serves 12.

Michael Morava, Superintendent, Fort Robinson State Park

This recipe was taken from the 1933 cookbook All About Home Baking *to be served at Fort Robinson State Park at the annual Christmas dinner. Each December, Fort Rob hosts a dinner based on an actual year that the Army served Christmas dinner to the troops stationed there from 1874 to 1948. Menus, decorations, and entertainment for the dinners are prepared to be as close as possible to the year celebrated.*

Pies, Pastries & Desserts

Ostkaka is a Swedish dessert that is a type of cheesecake or custard, which is not as creamy as the cheesecake that you may be accustomed to. Those that have grown up with it love it and continue the tradition of preparing it at Christmas time.

Ostkaka (Swedish Custard)

1 gallon homogenized milk
1 cup flour
1 tablet rennet
3 eggs beaten
1 teaspoon salt
1 cup sugar
1 cup whipping cream
1 Tablespoon vanilla

Heat 1 gallon of milk to lukewarm. Remove from heat. Make a thin paste of 1 cup flour mixed with a little cold milk. Add the paste to the warm milk and stir. Crush 1 tablet rennet and add 2 tablespoons of water. Stir and add to the milk-and-flour mixture. Stir with a spatula and let stand 45 minutes or until set. When set, cut through with spatula. Whey will form, and you can start to ladle the whey off or strain in a colander or sieve of cheesecloth. Do not drain dry, but leave a little whey on the curds. The curds will look like cottage cheese. Let the curds stand for a while until they become a little firmer, then add the 3 beaten eggs, 1 teaspoon salt, 1 cup sugar, 1 cup whipping cream, and 1 Tablespoon vanilla to them. Fold these ingredients in until mixed. Pour into baking dish and top with dabs of butter. Bake at 350° for 1 to 1 1/2 hours. After ostkaka is baked, run a knife around the outer edge between the ostkaka and pan to keep the center from falling. Serve warm with whipped cream and lingonberries. If you have access to fresh, nonpasteurized milk, that is what "old" Swedes and I prefer.

Senator Joel Johnson

Pies, Pastries & Desserts

Hot Fruit Casserole

1 can sliced pineapple
1 can peach halves
1 can pitted dark cherries
1 can pear halves
1 can apricots
1 stick butter or margarine
2 teaspoons flour
1/2 cup brown sugar
1/2 cup sherry

Drain fruit and layer in casserole dish. Place butter in skillet and melt over low heat. Add flour and mix until smooth. Lift the pan from the heat and stir in brown sugar. When smooth, add the sherry. Continue to heat, stirring constantly until it boils and thickens. Pour over fruit and refrigerate overnight. Heat at 350° until it starts to bubble.

Former Senator LaVon Crosby

This versatile recipe was adapted from the 1970 edition of the Congressional Club Cookbook, *submitted by Mrs. Sam Ervin Jr. I have made a few changes in the ingredients, but it remains a favorite because it can be used in so many ways: as a side dish with meat, an ice cream topping, or as dessert.*

Pies, Pastries & Desserts

The original back patio.

Cakes, Cookies & Candy

The Sun Porch

During the remodeling of the Residence, the back patio was transformed into a Sun Porch that could be used year-round. Adjacent to the Sun Porch, a patio was added that leads to the backyard, where many outdoor events are hosted.

The Heritage Room is home to the First Ladies' Doll Collection.
For more information on the collection, see page 214.

Cakes, Cookies & Candy

Angel-Food Cake

12 eggs
1 1/2 teaspoons cream of tartar
1/4 teaspoon salt
1 teaspoon vanilla
1/2 teaspoon almond flavoring
1 cup cake flour
1 1/2 cups sugar

Separate eggs (12 eggs at room temperature usually make 1 1/2 cups of whites) and add to the whites the cream of tartar, salt, vanilla, and almond flavoring.

Sift cake flour together with 3/4 cup sugar, 4 times.

Beat whites at low speed (to mix flavorings) and then at high speed until stiff yet moist.

At low speed, blend in 3/4 cup sugar with mixer. By hand, fold in flour mixture (folding counterclockwise, by fourths of bowl, small amount at a time.

Gently push batter into (very clean) angel-food pan. Slowly slice butter knife through mixture to settle air bubbles.

Bake at 375° for 30 to 35 minutes. Listen to cake to test for doneness. If it's still making sounds, put back in oven for about 5 minutes. Cool upside down.

The best frosting to retain the cake's flavor is simply softened butter, powdered sugar, 1 cap of vanilla, and enough whole milk to make it spreadable.

Former First Lady Ruth Thone

This recipe came out of the cake-flour box and now I think it's committed to memory. We use this cake for all the family birthdays and other times throughout the year as "unbirthday" occasions arise.

Cakes, Cookies & Candy

I was always trying to not eat sweets when I got to the "Mansion," but they served this coconut cake that was fabulous! One day they served a banana cake; I was only going to eat one bite, but it was warm and I finished the whole piece. The chef also had an apple goodie recipe that was to die for! So, not eating sweets at the Mansion was very difficult!

Coconut Cake

1 package yellow cake mix, prepared according to package directions
1 can cream of coconut
1 can Eagle Brand Sweetened Condensed Milk
1 carton whipping cream, whipped
Coconut flakes

Bake cake according to package direction in a 9 × 13-inch pan. When done, poke holes in cake with a fork. Pour the can of condensed milk and can of cream of coconut over the cake. Let cool. Spread the whipped cream over the cake then sprinkle with coconut flakes.

Former First Lady Stephanie Johanns

Sourdough Chocolate Cake

Combine the following ingredients in a large bowl and allow to set and bubble in a warm place for 2 hours:

2/3 cup Sourdough Starter (This & That, page 306)
1 cup lukewarm water
1 1/4 cups unsifted flour
1/4 cup dry milk

Sift together:

1 cup sugar
1/2 cup cocoa
1/2 teaspoon cinnamon
1 1/2 teaspoon soda
1/2 teaspoon salt

Add **2/3 cup shortening** to the dry ingredients. Mix until crumbly. Add **2 eggs** and **1 teaspoon vanilla**. Beat well. Add sourdough mixture. Beat until light and fluffy, about 2 minutes. Pour into 3 greased layer pans or one 9 × 13-inch pan. Bake layers 20 minutes or one large pan 30 minutes in a 350° oven.

LeeAnn Merrihew

This easy cake can be started and set aside for a couple of hours, and I can multitask another project or even do errands and come back to finish without a problem.

Cakes, Cookies & Candy

Lady Baltimore Cake

3/4 cup butter or other shortening
2 cups sugar
3 cups sifted cake flour
3 teaspoons baking powder
1/2 teaspoon salt
1/2 cup milk
1/2 cup water
1 teaspoon vanilla
6 egg whites

Cream shortening and sugar together until fluffy. Sift flour, baking powder, and salt together 3 times. Combine milk, water, and vanilla. Add small amounts of flour to creamed mixture, alternating with milk mixture, beating until smooth after each addition. Beat egg whites until stiff but not dry and fold into mixture. Pour into cake pans lined with waxed paper. Bake in moderate oven 350° for 25 minutes. Makes 3 (9-inch) layers.

Lady Baltimore Frosting and Filling

3 cups sugar
1 cup water
1/4 teaspoon cream of tartar
3 egg whites, stiffly beaten
1 teaspoon vanilla
1/2 cup chopped figs
1 cup chopped raisins
1 cup chopped nut meats

Boil sugar, water, and cream of tartar together to 238° or until a small amount of syrup will form a soft ball when tested in cold water. Pour hot syrup gradually over beaten egg whites, beating constantly and continuing until mixture is of spreading consistency. Add vanilla. Divide mixture in half. Add fruit and nuts to 1 portion and spread between layers of cake. Frost top and sides with remaining frosting.

From the kitchen of Bess Streeter Aldrich

The family room on the second floor of the new Residence, along with a small snack kitchen, gives the governor's family some privacy. Mrs. Fred Sieman, daughter of Governor Keith Neville (1917–1919), once said, "Living in the Mansion can often be like living in a fishbowl."

For years my family baked what we called "quetcha" kuchen, thinking quetcha were plums. Once, I was talking about quetcha kuchen with an elderly lady in Neligh, and she set me straight. It turns out the name is "quancha" kuchen, quancha meaning "gossip." This is a cake that would have been taken to a "Kaffee Klatch" where the ladies gossiped. So our quetcha kuchen turned out to be our "gossip" cake.

Italian Prune Cake

1 cup flour
1 teaspoon baking powder
1/2 teaspoon salt
1 egg
1/2 cup sugar
1/4 cup milk
2 Tablespoons oil
18 to 20 blue Italian plums
1/2 cup sugar
1/2 teaspoon cinnamon

Combine flour, baking powder, and salt in small bowl and set aside. In medium-sized bowl, mix egg and sugar until lemon-colored. In separate bowl, mix milk and oil. Add flour mixture and milk mixture alternately to egg mixture. Pour into greased 8-inch square pan. Cut plums in half, removing pit. Arrange cut sides on top of batter. Sprinkle with sugar and cinnamon. Bake in 350° oven for 40 minutes.

Mary Mahoney

Chocolate Zucchini Cake

4 eggs
2 cups grated zucchini
3/4 cup oil
1 teaspoon vanilla
4 1/2 ounces instant chocolate pudding mix, dry
1 package chocolate cake mix
1 package semisweet chocolate chips (optional)
Frosting (optional)

Grease cake pan or make into cupcakes. Preheat oven according to package directions. Beat eggs, zucchini, oil, vanilla, and pudding mix. Add cake mix, beat on medium speed for 5 to 10 minutes. Pour into cake pan. (In place of frosting, pour the package of chocolate chips on before baking cake.) Bake according to package. If you are using frosting, let cake stand 10 minutes before frosting. (Do not use frosting if you put chocolate chips on cake.)

This is a very moist cake. Refrigerate leftovers.

Dianna Jensen

This recipe became a very big hit in our family. My then elementary-aged nephew would go to grandma and grandpa's house after school. Grandma would always have a "lunch" for the grandkids to eat before they were off playing with friends. On this particular day, chocolate zucchini cupcakes were for lunch. My nephew began eating and immediately pulled out pieces of grated zucchini. He said, "Grandma, these cupcakes have weeds in them." But he kept right on eating the cupcakes.

Zucchini nearly grows wild in Nebraska and so this recipe has definitely filled a place for all the zucchini at our house. This is our all-time favorite cake, and with a little dollop of whipped topping, it is a real winner.

Chocolate Chip Zucchini Cake

1/2 cup oil
1/4 cup margarine
1 3/4 cups sugar
2 eggs
1 teaspoon vanilla
2 1/2 cups flour
4 Tablespoons cocoa
1/2 teaspoon salt
1/2 teaspoon cinnamon
1/2 cup sour milk
1 teaspoon soda
2 cups grated zucchini

Topping

1 cup chocolate chips
2 Tablespoons white sugar
1/2 cup chopped nuts
2 Tablespoons brown sugar

Mix together oil and margarine, add sugar and blend. Add eggs and vanilla. Beat well. Sift flour, cocoa, salt, and cinnamon; add milk. Beat well. Blend in zucchini. Pour into greased 9 × 13-inch pan. Before baking, mix together the topping ingredients. Sprinkle on top of cake and bake at 350° for 45 to 50 minutes.

Alice Dubs

Karithopita (Walnut Cake)

12 eggs, separated
2 cups powdered sugar
12 zwieback toast, pulverized
3 cups ground walnuts
1 teaspoon cinnamon
1/2 teaspoon cloves
1/2 teaspoon nutmeg
1/2 pound butter
1 teaspoon baking powder

For Syrup:
2 cups water
2 cups sugar
1 lemon slice
1 orange slice
1 cinnamon stick
1 cup honey

Beat egg yolks and powdered sugar; add toast, nuts, and spices. Mix. Beat egg whites and fold in (do not beat in). Bake 350° about 30 to 35 minutes or until toothpick comes out clean. Cool cake before pouring on syrup.

Syrup

Boil water, sugar, lemon, orange, and cinnamon for 15 minutes or until thermometer reads 250°. Add honey after it begins to boil; allow to boil for 5 more minutes. Pour slowly over cake.

Deb Kildow

This cake is served with Sunday dinner at the Greek Festival in Bridgeport, Nebraska. Pronounced Ka (short a) de (long e) do (long o, emphasis on the do) pe (long e) ta (short a), this is a walnut cake drenched in honey syrup.

Cakes, Cookies & Candy

This recipe came from my mother, Esther (Coleman) Drinkwalter, through my sister, Charlotte. This cake was always made on my birthday in duplicate for my brother and myself. We always asked for the same kind of cake and always got our own cake to eat.

Applesauce Cake

1 3/4 cups flour
1 teaspoon baking powder
1/2 teaspoon salt
1/2 teaspoon nutmeg
1 1/2 teaspoons cinnamon
1/4 teaspoon cloves
1 cup firmly packed brown sugar
1/2 cup shortening
1 egg
1 1/2 cups applesauce
1 cup raisins

Sift dry ingredients. Beat brown sugar, shortening, and eggs in 3-quart bowl until light and fluffy. Mix in dry ingredients alternately with applesauce. Stir in raisins. Pour into greased 8-inch square pan. Bake 45 minutes or until toothpick comes out clean. Serve immediately afterwards or cool. May sift powdered sugar lightly over top.

Lois Keim

Cakes, Cookies & Candy

Best Chocolate Cake

In a large bowl, mix:

2 cups sugar
2 cups flour
1/4 teaspoon salt

In a saucepan:

2 sticks butter, melted
1 cup water
4 Tablespoons cocoa

Bring to a boil and add to the above dry ingredients. Mix well. Add **2 eggs**, **1/4 cup milk**, **1 teaspoon vanilla**, and **1 Tablespoon vinegar**. Fold in **1 teaspoon vanilla**. Pour into a 9 × 13-inch oiled and floured pan. Bake at 350° for 25 minutes. Cool before frosting.

Cooked Frosting

In a saucepan on the stove, melt **3/4 stick of butter**. Add **6 Tablespoons milk** and **4 Tablespoons cocoa powder**. Bring to a boil and add **1 pound powdered sugar** and stir until smooth. Add **4 teaspoons vanilla**, stir, and let sit until cool. Pour over cake and spread smooth.

Senator Jim and Patricia A. Jones

We live on the Ash Creek Ranch south of Broken Bow, near Eddyville, Nebraska. This was my mother's recipe, and she made this seven times in eleven days when Jim and I were on a trip celebrating our twenty-fifth wedding anniversary. She made this for my father and son who were caring for the ranch while we were gone.

This was my family's favorite request at birthdays.

Waldorf-Astoria Red Velvet Cake

1/2 cup shortening
1 1/2 cups sugar
2 eggs
2 ounces red food coloring (1/4 cup)
2 heaping teaspoons cocoa
1 cup buttermilk
2 1/2 cups cake flour
1 teaspoon salt
1 teaspoon vanilla
1 teaspoon baking soda
1 teaspoon vinegar

Cream shortening, sugar, and eggs. Make paste of food coloring and cocoa. Add to creamed mixture. Add buttermilk with flour and salt. Add vanilla. Add baking soda to vinegar (hold over bowl as it foams). Blend in baking soda and vinegar mixture. Bake in 2 8-inch greased and floured layer pans. Bake 25 to 30 minutes. Cut each layer in half.

Frosting

3 teaspoons flour
1 cup milk
1 cup sugar

1 cup butter
1 teaspoon vanilla

Cook flour and milk until thick, stirring constantly, then cool. Cream sugar, butter, and vanilla until fluffy. Blend into milk-and-flour mixture and spread.

Senator Vicki McDonald

Cakes, Cookies & Candy

Carrot Cake

4 eggs
2 cups sugar
1 1/4 cups canola oil
2 cups all-purpose flour
2 teaspoons soda
1 teaspoon cinnamon
1/2 teaspoon salt
1/2 teaspoon nutmeg
3 cups raw shredded carrots
1 cup nuts (optional)
1/2 cup raisins (optional)

Beat eggs. Combine sugar and oil and add to eggs. Sift dry ingredients together and mix in. Add carrots and other optional ingredients as desired. Bake at 325° to 350° for 45 minutes or until toothpick comes out clean.

Frosting

1/4 cup butter
1/2 teaspoon vanilla
3 ounces cream cheese
1 1/2 cups powdered sugar
1/8 teaspoon salt

Cream together all ingredients. Spread over cake.

State Auditor Mike Foley

This carrot cake is one of Auditor Foley's favorites and is usually used for his birthday cake.

A similar recipe was submitted by Vicki Bromm.

Les Gateaux

Chocolate Batter

1 1/2 cups flour
1/4 cup cocoa
1/2 teaspoon salt
1 cup water
1/3 cup oil
1 cup sugar
1 teaspoon soda
1 Tablespoon vinegar
1 teaspoon vanilla

Filling

1 (8-ounce) package cream cheese
1/3 cup sugar
1 egg
1 cup chocolate chips

Mix filling ingredients together. Beat chocolate batter until well combined. Fill muffin cups 1/3 full of chocolate batter and add 1 heaping Tablespoon cream cheese filling. Bake at 350° for 20 minutes. Makes 24.

Variations: Add food coloring to the cream cheese filling or use mint-flavored chocolate chips instead of regular chocolate chips.

Senator Ed and Judy Schrock

Chocolate Chip Oatmeal Cookies (Famous FHS Pressbox Cookies)

1 cup butter-flavored Crisco
3/4 cup white sugar
3/4 cup brown sugar
2 eggs
1 tablespoon vanilla
1 teaspoon salt
1 teaspoon soda
 2 cups oatmeal (quick)
1 to 1 1/2 cups flour
1 to 1 1/2 cups chocolate chips

Cream together the Crisco, sugars, eggs, vanilla, salt, and soda until very pale brown. Beat in the oatmeal and 1 cup flour. Stir in the chocolate chips (the more, the better). Add more flour until not real sticky, but not dry. Drop by teaspoons onto ungreased cookie sheets. Bake at 350° for 10 to 12 minutes until they begin to brown. Check at 10 minutes. Remove from oven and drop cookie sheet on top of stove to make the cookies "fall." Cookies that are too browned or whose dough was too dry will not have a "chewy" texture. Let cool on cookie sheet for about 5 minutes before removing to a rack. I like to store these in the refrigerator to keep them fresh. Makes 4 dozen.

Wanda Samson

As of 2007, I have worked thirty-four years in the pressbox of Fremont High School compiling the results for the track meets. One year I decided to bring a batch of these chocolate chip cookies for the workers to enjoy. This became a habit!

M&M Coconut Macaroon Cookies

3 cups coconut, sweetened flaked (packed, like brown sugar)
3/4 cup sweetened condensed milk
1 teaspoon vanilla
3/4 cup chocolate chips or Mini M&M's

Mix all together and drop by teaspoon on a well greased cookie sheet. Bake at 350°. Remove from pan immediately and let cool on rack. Store at room temperature. Makes 3 dozen.

Sandy Austin

Candy Bar Cookies

20 Popsicle sticks
1 bag Fun Size Snickers
1/2 cup sugar
1/2 cup brown sugar
1/2 cup butter
1/2 cup peanut butter
1 teaspoon vanilla
1 egg
1 1/2 cup flour
1/2 teaspoon baking powder
1/2 teaspoon baking soda
1/4 teaspoon salt

Mix sugars, butter, peanut butter, vanilla, and egg. Add flour and dry ingredients. Mix into a soft dough. Take approximately 1/3 cup dough and form around a Snickers candy bar. Place dough-covered bars 4 inches apart on an ungreased cookie sheet. Bake at 350° for 13 to 16 minutes or until golden brown. For a wonderful cookie for a more mature audience, you may delete the sticks.

Senator Dwite Pederson

Remember the day when you celebrated your birthday by bringing treats for all your classmates? This cookie recipe is the one I made for my children to share.

Cakes, Cookies & Candy

Mexican Wedding Cookies (Cuernitos)

1/2 cup powdered sugar
1 cup butter, softened
2 teaspoons almond extract
1 teaspoon vanilla extract
2 cups flour
1/4 teaspoon salt
1 cup finely chopped almonds or pecans

Preheat oven to 325°. In a large bowl, beat powdered sugar, butter, and extracts until light and fluffy. Stir in flour, salt, and almonds or pecans. Mix until dough forms. Shape into 1-inch balls. The cookies should be the size of a quarter. Place on ungreased cookie sheet. Bake at 325° for 15 to 20 minutes. Watch closely until set but not brown. Remove from cookie sheet, cool slightly, and roll in powdered sugar. Let cool completely and roll again in powdered sugar.

Tomas Rojas

Oatmeal Cranberry
White Chocolate Chunk Cookies

2/3 cup butter or margarine, softened
2/3 cup brown sugar
2 large eggs
1 1/2 cups old-fashioned oats
1 1/2 cups flour
1 teaspoon baking soda
1/2 teaspoon salt
6 ounces Craisins Sweetened Dried Cranberries
2/3 cup white chocolate chunks or chips

Preheat oven to 375°. Using electric mixer, beat butter or margarine and sugar together in a medium mixing bowl until light and fluffy. Add eggs, mixing well. Combine oats, flour, baking soda, and salt in a separate mixing bowl. Add to butter mixture in several additions, mixing well after each addition. Stir in sweetened, dried cranberries and white chocolate chunks. Drop by rounded teaspoonful onto ungreased cookie sheet. Bake 10 to 12 minutes or until golden brown. Makes approximately 2 1/2 dozen cookies.

Kristi Leckband

When my children were little, one of the things we enjoyed doing together was making cookies. My husband had died in an auto accident and even though I was working full time, we had very little money. Our fun activities were sewing doll clothes, flying kites, and making cookies.

Senator Howard's Lace Cookies

1 cup sifted flour
1 cup chopped flaked coconut or chopped walnuts
1/2 cup light corn syrup
1/2 cup firmly packed brown sugar
1/2 cup butter or margarine
1 teaspoon vanilla

Heat oven to 350°. Mix flour and coconut (or walnuts). Combine light corn syrup, brown sugar, and butter or margarine in heavy saucepan. Over medium heat, bring syrup mixture to a boil, stirring constantly. Remove from heat. Gradually blend flour mixture, then vanilla, into syrup mixture. Drop onto foil-covered cookie sheets by scant teaspoon 3 inches apart (dough will spread during baking). Cool on wire rack until foil peels easily. Remove foil and place cookies on rack covered with absorbent paper.

Senator Gwen Howard

Cakes, Cookies & Candy

Drop Sugar Cookies

2 1/2 cups sifted all-purpose flour
1/2 teaspoon baking soda
1/2 teaspoon salt
1/2 cup room-temperature butter
1/2 cup shortening
1 cup sugar
1 teaspoon vanilla
1 egg
2 Tablespoons milk

Preheat oven to 350°. Combine all dry ingredients in a large mixing bowl. Cream together the butter, shortening, and sugar. Add the vanilla, egg, and milk to butter, then mix with the dry mixture. Use a tablespoon to drop the batter onto a greased cookie sheet, allowing an inch for spreading. Bake 10 minutes or until the cookies are light gold at the edges.

Attorney General Jon Bruning

Anise Cookies

3 eggs
1 cup sugar
1 1/2 cups flour
1 teaspoon baking powder
1/4 teaspoon anise oil
1/2 teaspoon lemon extract

Beat the eggs until very light. Add the sugar gradually, beating well after each addition; add flavorings. Sift together flour and baking powder and add gradually to egg and sugar mixture using a wire eggbeater. Drop by half spoonfuls onto well-greased and floured cookie sheets about 1 inch apart. Let stand in the kitchen overnight to dry. Bake for about 5 minutes in a moderate oven. Makes about 7 dozen bite-size cookies. Can be made bigger.

Edith Stranberg
Submitted by Sharon Cimpel

Chocolate Chip Oatmeal Cookies

3/4 cup white sugar
3/4 cup brown sugar
1 cup butter (or margarine)
2 eggs
1 teaspoon vanilla

Cream together and add the following:

2 cups all-purpose flour
1 teaspoon baking powder
1 teaspoon baking soda
2 cups oatmeal
1 cup chocolate chips

Mix together as for any cookie. Bake at 350° on greased sheets for 10 minutes.

Jolene Ward

As a young bride, when it came time to bake simple chocolate chip cookies for the first time as a married lady, I didn't have any reservations. Imagine my surprise when my new hubby took one bite, shrugged his shoulders, and said, "Maybe you should call my mother and get her recipe." This is Mother Ward's recipe.

My grandmother always had a big glass jar on the kitchen table filled with these cookies. Grandpa loved them with coffee, and we grandchildren loved them with milk.

Grandma O's White Crisp Cookies

3 cups flour
1 cup shortening
1 teaspoon baking soda
1/2 teaspoon salt
2 teaspoons baking powder

Mix as you would for pie crust with a pastry blender.

Add:

1 cup sugar
2 eggs, slightly beaten
4 Tablespoons milk
1 teaspoon vanilla

Mix together by hand. Roll thin; cut with cookie cutter. Bake at 400° 10 to 12 minutes. Sprinkle with colored sugar before baking or frost with powdered sugar icing. Makes 3 1/2 dozen.

Carol (Portenier) Yelken

Pumpkin Chocolate Chip Cookies

2 cups flour
1 cup oatmeal
1 teaspoon cinnamon
1/2 teaspoon salt
1 cup oleo
1 cup sugar
1 cup brown sugar
1 egg
1 teaspoon vanilla
1 cup pumpkin
1 cup chocolate chips

Mix together well and drop on cookie sheet. Bake 350° for 15 to 20 minutes.

Jaynette Keim

I have made these since November 1985, and my sons look for them each holiday. I also have a very dear friend that always enjoys them each time I share with her.

Danish Sugar Cookies

1 cup butter
1 cup sugar
1 egg
1/2 teaspoon baking powder
2 cups white flour
1/2 teaspoon cream of tartar
1 teaspoon nutmeg
1 teaspoon vanilla

Cream together butter and sugar. Add egg and dry ingredients. Chill in refrigerator 30 minutes. Make small balls. Roll each in sugar, put on cookie sheet, and press down. Bake at 350° for 8 minutes.

Jan Rojewski

Sugar Cookies

Cream until fluffy:

1 cup butter
1 cup vegetable oil
1 cup powdered sugar
1 cup white sugar

Add:

2 eggs, beaten
1 teaspoon vanilla

Sift together:

4 cups flour
1 teaspoon soda
1 teaspoon cream of tartar
1 teaspoon salt

Add dry ingredients to creamed mixture and chill well. Roll 1 teaspoon of dough and press down lightly with glass dipped in sugar. Bake at 375° for 11 minutes. Serves several grandchildren.

Barb Hansen

These are the lightest sugar cookies you will ever find.

My mother taught me to make these at a young age, and they became one of my favorites!

Lemon Crisscross Cookies

1/2 cup shortening (part butter or margarine)
3/4 cup sugar
1 egg
1/2 teaspoon lemon extract
1 3/4 cups flour
3/4 teaspoon cream of tartar
3/4 teaspoon baking soda
1/4 teaspoon salt
1 cup raisins

Heat oven to 400°. Mix shortening, sugar, egg, and lemon extract. Blend flour, cream of tartar, baking soda, and salt. Stir into shortening mixture. Mix in raisins. Roll into 1-inch balls. Place about 3 inches apart on ungreased baking sheet. Flatten with a fork dipped in flour, making a crisscross pattern. Bake 8 to 10 minutes. Makes about 3 dozen cookies.

Gerry Oligmueller

Mrs. Heine's Oatmeal Raisin Cookies

Cream together the following:

1/2 cup butter
1 cup white sugar
2 eggs
1/2 cup milk

Add:

1 teaspoon baking powder
1/2 teaspoon salt
1 1/2 teaspoon cinnamon
2 cups oatmeal
1 1/2 cups raisins

Bake at 350° for 8 to 10 minutes.

Senator Danielle Nantkes

Mrs. Heine was Senator Nantkes' third- and fourth-grade teacher in Staplehurst, Nebraska.

Frosted Rhubarb Cookies

1 cup shortening
1 1/2 cups brown sugar
2 eggs
3 cups flour
1 teaspoon baking soda
1/2 teaspoon salt
1 1/2 cups diced rhubarb
3/4 cup coconut

Cream the shortening and sugar. Add eggs and blend well. Combine flour, baking soda, and salt. Add to creamed mixture. Stir in rhubarb and coconut. Drop onto cookie sheets and bake at 350° for 10 to 12 minutes. Frost with cream cheese frosting while still warm.

Cream Cheese Frosting

3 ounces cream cheese
1 Tablespoon butter
1 teaspooon vanilla
1 1/2 cups powdered sugar

Combine the cream cheese and butter until fluffy. Add vanilla. Add powdered sugar and beat until smooth.

Cornelia Kliewer

Gingersnaps

3/4 cup shortening
1 cup light brown sugar, packed
1/4 cup molasses
1 egg
2 cups flour
2 teaspoons baking soda
1 teaspoon cinnamon
1 teaspoon cloves
1 teaspoon ginger

Cream together shortening, light brown sugar, molasses, and egg. Add flour, baking soda, cinnamon, cloves, and ginger. Blend well. Roll into ball and place on cookie sheet. Flatten with bottom of glass dipped in sugar. Bake at 375° for 8 to 10 minutes.

Tina Larson

One of the traditional Christmas recipes in our family is peppernuts, a small, hard spice cookie. Christmas is not the same without them.

Peppernuts

3 cups syrup, light if you want light peppernuts or use half light and half dark
2 Tablespoons soda, dissolved in a little cold water
Grated rind and juice of 2 lemons
1 pound butter or margarine, softened
2 cups sugar
4 eggs, beaten
1 teaspoon salt
2 Tablespoons ground anise seed or 1/2 teaspoon anise oil
2 Tablespoons cinnamon
1 Tablespoon cardamon
1 Tablespoon cloves
Flour to make very stiff dough, about 5 pounds
1/2 pound peanuts, chopped (optional)

Grate lemon rinds. Squeeze juice out. Add syrup in large bowl. Stir well. Cream butter and sugar; beat in eggs and salt. Add dissolved soda a little at a time to syrup in large bowl. Stir to keep it from foaming over. Add syrup mixture to creamed butter mixture. Beat well. Add anise oil if that is what you are using. Mix spices with 1 1/2 cups to 2 cups flour. Blend well. Beat into above mixture. Stir in rest of flour. It will take 5 pounds in all. Cover tightly and refrigerate overnight. Would be all right for several days if tightly covered. Roll in small balls. Bake on greased cookie sheets until lightly browned at 375°.

If lemons are large, cut the juice to about 1/2 cup.

Mrs. Dean (Karen) Hawthorne

Cakes, Cookies & Candy

Salted Nut Roll

2 cups miniature marshmallows
1 (10-ounce) package peanut butter chips
1 can sweetened condensed milk
3 1/2 Tablespoons butter or margarine
1 (20-ounce) jar of dry roasted peanuts

Butter 9 × 13-inch pan. In large saucepan, melt peanut butter chips and butter. Stir until well mixed and smooth. Remove from heat and add milk and marshmallows. Stir until smooth. Spread 1/2 jar peanuts in bottom of pan. Pour mixture over nuts. Cover with remaining 1/2 jar peanuts. Refrigerate until cooled. Cut into squares.

Deanna Ray

Peanut Butter Balls

1/2 cup peanut butter
1 cup powdered sugar
3 Tablespoons butter
1 cup Rice Krispies
Chocolate almond bark, melted

Mix all ingredients, except chocolate almond bark, and refrigerate. Shape into balls. Cover with melted chocolate almond bark.

Kristi Leckband

Salted Nut Rolls are my dad's favorite candy bar and this was the closest thing to them.

This fudge recipe came about after I found a recipe in the Omaha World-Herald *that Mamie Eisenhower said was Ike's favorite.*

Janie's Fudge

In a large, heat-resistant bowl (5- to 6-quart), mix the following ingredients and set aside:

**4 to 4 1/2 cups real semisweet chocolate chips
(sets a little faster with 4 1/2 cups; you may substitute some grated butterscotch chips for a milder fudge)
3 1/2 cups mini marshmallows or 1 (7-ounce) jar of marshmallow creme
1 cup to 1 pound nuts (chopped or whole; optional)**

In a smaller container, place the amount of nuts you want to stir in later. If I'm going to drop the fudge into petite cups, I chop the nuts or sometimes stick them into the top whole. Butter or spray a 9 × 13-inch pan that you'll pour the fudge into.

In a 3-quart heavy saucepan, or one that is not likely to scorch, place the following ingredients:

**4 1/2 cups granulated sugar or equal mixture of white and brown sugar
1 (13- to 15-ounce) can evaporated milk
2 Tablespoons butter or margarine
Dash of salt**

Cook the above 4 ingredients over a low enough heat that you won't scorch the sugar mixture, stirring often. After the mixture starts to boil, time the cooking for 6 to 7 minutes. Remove from stove and pour over the chip/marshmallow mixture. Stir the ingredients until creamy smooth. Stir in the nuts and continue to stir until the mixture starts to set up. Pour into pan.

Cakes, Cookies & Candy

Usually at this point I make the petite candy or muffin cups by using teaspoons or a small scoop to drop amounts into the petite cups. I also have left out the nuts, poured the fudge onto flat pans, and use cookie cutters to cut seasonal designs.

Mary Jane Bell

In 1958, the interior of the Residence was decorated in five complementary styles: French Provincial (1690–1792), Georgian (1715–1753), Louis XVI (1760–1790), Empire (1804–1815), and Regency (1800–1830).

Cakes, Cookies & Candy

Peanut Butter Fantasy Fudge

3 cups sugar
3/4 cup Parkay margarine
2/3 cup (6-ounce can) evaporated milk
1 cup chunky or creamy Jif peanut butter
2 cups (7-ounce jar) marshmallow creme
1 cup peanuts, chopped
1 teaspoon vanilla

Combine sugar, margarine, and milk; bring to rolling boil. Cook rapidly 5 minutes over medium heat, stirring constantly (mixture scorches easily). Remove from heat, stir in peanut butter. Add marshmallow creme, peanuts, and vanilla; beat until well blended. Pour into greased 9 × 13-inch pan. Cool before cutting into squares.

Darlene Davis

Pralines

2 cups sugar
1 cup brown sugar
1 stick oleo
Pinch of salt
2 Tablespoons Karo Syrup
1 small (12-ounce) can evaporated milk

Mix all and cook to a "soft ball." Cool a little.

Add:

1 teaspoon vanilla

Beat and add:

2 cups pecans

Drop by spoonfuls onto waxed paper to cool.

Senator Russ and Jill Karpisek

This is my favorite "Southern recipe." My Grandma Katie, who grew up in Louisiana, has been making pralines since she was a little girl. Whenever they would visit us in Nebraska, she would always bring us a large container of pralines, and they were usually all gone in two days! It has taken me a couple of batches to get them to turn out as good as Grandma's ... the key is patience. The pralines need to cool before the vanilla is added and then beaten. If they are not cooled enough, they get too gooey when spooned onto the waxed paper.

The original Front Drive.

This & That

The Front Drive

The Front Drive was built to give elegant and easy access to the front door of the Residence for the First Family and visitors. As the grounds have been developed over the years, the exterior continues to feature the circular drive through the remote-controlled gates. Additionally, the front entrance has been made ADA accessible.

The east pathway on the Residence grounds provides a scenic view of the Capitol.

The fountain in the backyard of the Residence was added during the renovation of the grounds.

This & That

Pinezucot Jam or Cranzu-Raspberry Jam

6 cups grated, peeled zucchini
1/2 cup water
6 cups sugar
2 Tablespoons lemon juice
1 pound can crushed pineapple
2 small boxes Jell-O (apricot or cran-raspberry)

Bring grated zucchini and water to a boil in a large pan. Boil gently for 6 minutes; stir to keep from burning. Drain and add sugar, lemon juice, and pineapple. Bring to a boil for 6 minutes, then stir. Add gelatin and boil 2 minutes, then stir. Have hot sterilized jars and lids ready in water-bath pan. Ladle jam into hot jars, wipe edge clean, put on hot lids, screw down, and turn over for 5 minutes. Turn jam right side up. Lids will snap and seal.

Sharon Ann Loudon, Ellsworth

I created these names for the best jam recipe to use with overgrown zucchini. These jams, along with others, are added to my holiday baskets that I have been giving to family and friends for years. You can switch and add cranberry-raspberry Jell-O to serve at Christmas and keep the apricot for Thanksgiving. This recipe is easy for a first-time canner.

Jalapeño Hot Pepper Jelly

1/2 cup jalapeño peppers, seeded
3/4 cup ground bell pepper
6 1/2 cups sugar
1 1/3 cups cider vinegar
1 (6- to 7-ounce) bottle liquid pectin
Red food coloring

Mix peppers, sugar, and vinegar in a saucepan. Bring to a rolling boil. Remove from heat and let set 5 minutes. Stir well. Add pectin and food coloring; mix thoroughly. Ladle hot jelly into hot, sterilized pint jars, leaving 1/4-inch head space. Adjust two-piece caps (seal and ring). Process 10 minutes in boiling water canner. Serve over creamed cheese on crackers. Makes 6 to 7 1/2 pints. Note: When cutting and seeding peppers, wear gloves to prevent burning.

Nancy Seeman

Ice Cream Topping

3 cups sugar
2/3 cup cocoa
1 (12-ounce) can evaporated milk
1/2 cup butter
1/2 cup peanut butter
1 teaspoon vanilla

In a saucepan, combine the sugar and cocoa. Add the evaporated milk. Heat to a boil and boil for 3 minutes, stirring constantly. Add butter, peanut butter, and vanilla. Serve warm. Store covered in refrigerator. Reheat in the microwave.

Evelyn May

Grandma Katie's Hot Mustard

1/2 cup flour
1/4 cup dry mustard
1/4 cup sugar

Mix together above dry ingredients, then add the following:

1/4 cup horseradish, drained (ground, not cream-style)
1/4 cup regular table mustard
1/2 cup half-and-half

Mix all together and refrigerate. It keeps well. Serve with ham or pork. It's also great drizzled over homemade ham-and-bean soup.

Senator Pat Engel

Honey and Oats Granola

2 to 3 pounds rolled oats
2 cups shredded coconut
2 cups dried roasted nuts or seeds (peanuts, sunflower seeds, etc.)
2 cups wheat germ
1 Tablespoon salt
1 1/2 cups vegetable oil
1 1/2 cups honey
3 Tablespoons of vanilla
2/3 cup of water

Mix dry ingredients with moist ingredients. Stir well. Bake at 250° for 1 1/2 hours, stirring every 15 minutes. Add raisins.

Anita Wiechman

A similar recipe was contributed by Carmelee Tuma, Assistant to Governor Dave Heineman, who recommended the addition of cinnamon.

Homemade Noodles

2 eggs
1 Tablespoon butter or margarine, melted
2 Tablespoons heavy cream
1/2 teaspoon baking powder
1/4 teaspoon salt
Flour

Beat eggs. Add all other ingredients and beat again. Add flour, a cup at a time until too heavy to use mixer. Knead by hand until the mixture will not take flour. Divide into three portions. Roll until as thin as possible. Dry on a towel until surface is not sticky. Wrap each piece into a tight roll. Slice with a sharp knife as wide as desired. Cook or store in freezer.

Diann Jensen

Grandma's Noodles

After making your favorite pot of soup, let it simmer. In a small container, mix eggs with flour. Four eggs is a good number to begin the mixture. Use a fork to beat the eggs, then spoon flour in with a tablespoon and mix thoroughly. Keep adding flour by the Tablespoon until it is roughly the consistency of thick glue. Use the fork to scoop and drizzle the batter into the simmering soup. (The noodles cook very quickly.) Continue moving the noodles aside so you can place in the broth. If you need more room to put the noodles, they can also be cooked in simmering water.

Georgia Cronin

This is a recipe that was never written down. I learned it from my mom in the same way she learned it from her mom—by watching. My kids (at least three generations later) love these; they ask for them all the time and even fight over who gets the last ones. The funny thing is, when my mom was telling her mom how much my kids liked them, she laughed and said she didn't remember making them at all!

One of the first acts of Governor Ralph G. Brooks (1956–1960) upon entering office was to appoint his wife as official Residence receptionist. Her guest book shows a wide range of visitors. Senator John F. Kennedy said that the Residence and the Capitol were equal to any state government buildings he had seen. Actor Chuck Connors stated, "This marks the first time I've been in a Governor's Mansion, but it's hard to believe that any state could top this one."

When western Nebraska was being settled and land was available, homesteaders lived miles from towns located mostly along the railroads. In 1914, Josie Merrihew came to join her husband, bringing their children from Missouri and setting up housekeeping in a soddie thirteen miles from town. Yeast was hard to come by for rolls and bread, so they used potato water as a starter because everyone grew potatoes. Josie and her daughter-in-law, Dorothy (Mrs. Victor Merrihew), called their starter "Homer," and it made a nice, neighborly gift for new families to the Sandhills. You can feed and divide the starter, keeping it going for many months and dividing it into jars.

Sourdough Starter

Put the following ingredients in a large bowl (but never in a metal container):

2 cups warm potato water (saved from cooking peeled potatoes)
3 Tablespoons sugar
1/2 teaspoon salt
1 3/4 cups unsifted flour

Mix well. Cover and set bowl in a warm, draft-free spot. Allow the starter to work 12 to 24 hours before using it in your recipes. Makes 2 cups.
How to feed the starter:

Add to the original starter, which was left in the crock:

3/4 cup warm water
1 1/2 Tablespoons sugar
1/2 teaspoon sugar
7/8 cup flour

Set in a warm spot to work. After 3 or 4 hours, you can store in the refrigerator.

LeeAnn Merrihew

Sweet and Tangy Meat Sauce

1 jar chili sauce
1 can sauerkraut
1 cup brown sugar
1 cup white sugar
1/4 cup water
2 Tablespoons vinegar

Mix ingredients together. Add to previously prepared meatballs and heat in Crock-Pot for several hours.

Kathy Portrey

Governor Frank B. Morrison's (1961–1967) years in the Residence saw their complement of unusual events and visits. During the days of student activism in the '60s, the Residence was once filled with 600 students, who had come to call on the governor in his office. He invited them to return later that evening and talked to them until midnight.

Just Like Dorothy Lynch Dressing

1 cup vegetable oil
1 cup sugar
1 (10 3/4-ounce) can of tomato soup
1/2 cup cider vinegar
1 teaspoon celery seed
1 teaspoon salt
1 teaspoon pepper
2 teaspoons dry mustard
1/2 teaspoon garlic powder

Combine all ingredients in a blender. Mix on low speed until blended. Store in refrigerator.

Clara Loftus

Favorite Salad Dressing

1 cup oil
1/3 cup sugar
1/3 cup vinegar
1 small onion, quartered (or less)
1 Tablespoon prepared mustard
1 teaspoon celery seed
1/2 teaspoon salt
1/2 teaspoon pepper

Combine above ingredients and blend in blender. Make ahead and chill.

Mix the following ingredients to make the salad:

6 cups mixed salad greens
2 hard-boiled eggs, sliced
8 bacon strips, cooked and crumbled
Red onion rings

Pour salad dressing over greens.

Deb Lipinski

Poppy Seed Dressing

1/2 cup vinaigrette red wine dressing
1/2 cup sugar
1 teaspoon dry mustard
1/4 cup white vinegar
1 Tablespoon grated white onion
1/2 cup vegetable oil
1 Tablespoon poppy seeds

Mix well. Can use blender.

Mock Olive Garden Dressing

1 (8-ounce) bottle Paul Newman's Oil & Vinegar Dressing
2 Tablespoons grated Parmesan cheese
2 Tablespoons Wishbone Italian Dressing
2 teaspoons sugar
1/8 teaspoon dry mustard

Put all of above ingredients into a blender. Blend on high until smooth. Use sparingly on greens. Makes 1 pint.

Deb Lipinski

The backyard of the Residence is landscaped to provide a degree of privacy for the events held on the premises and a feeling of serenity.

This & That

The original Kitchen.

Complete Meals

The Kitchen

The Kitchen is used to prepare meals for the First Family, as well as the functions hosted in the Residence. When asked about memories of their time in the Residence, First Families always refer to the chef as part of their family. The chef for the Governor's Residence is Kathy Henning, featured on page 314.

The modern kitchen supports six ovens to handle meals for the large groups that use the Residence for events.

The kitchen cabinets include refrigerator drawers to provide additional refrigerated space.

Kathy Henning, chef at the Governor's Residence for official functions of the Governor, First Lady, and the many Nebraskans who come to the house.

Complete Meals

Governor's Residence
Breakfast Menu:

Homestyle Good Morning Casserole

Bran Muffins

Homestyle Good Morning Casserole

4 slices bread, crust trimmed
6 eggs
1 1/2 cups skim or low fat milk
4 slices cooked turkey bacon, crumbled
1/4 cup (1 ounce) shredded reduced fat cheddar cheese, divided
1/4 cup (1 ounce) shredded reduced fat Swiss cheese, divided
1/3 cup sliced mushrooms
1/4 teaspoon seasoned salt (optional)
1/2 cup frozen hash brown potatoes, thawed

Across bottom of lightly greased 9×9×2–inch baking dish, arrange bread slices, slightly overlapping. Set aside. In large bowl, beat together eggs, milk, bacon, 2 tablespoons each of Swiss and cheddar cheeses, mushrooms, and salt if desired. Pour mixture over bread slices; sprinkle potatoes and remaining cheeses over egg mixture. Cover and refrigerate overnight. Bake uncovered in preheated oven at 350° oven until lightly browned and knife inserted near center comes out clean (about 40 to 45 minutes).

Bran Muffins

Combine and set aside the following ingredients:

2 cups All Bran cereal
1 cup Bran Bud cereal
1 cup boiling water

Combine the following ingredients in a large bowl, and then mix with the cereal and water:

2 cups buttermilk
2 1/2 cups baking soda
1 cup honey
2 eggs, beaten
1/2 cup vegetable oil

Combine the following and then mix with moistened ingredients:

2 cups Miller Bran
1 cup whole wheat flour
1/2 cup white flour
1/2 teaspoon salt
1 cup chopped dates or raisins

Bake at 375° for 16 to 18 minutes.

Makes 28 muffins.

Karen Toussaint's (Governor's Residence Director) personal recipe—rquested by many.

Complete Meals

Another view of the formal place setting.

Complete Meals

Governor's Residence

Lunch Menu:

Chicken Salad

Fruit Garnish

Dinner Rolls

Chicken Salad

1 large cooked diced chicken breast (may substitute 1 can diced chicken or tuna)
1 cup frozen peas
1/2 cup chopped green onion
1/2 cup chopped celery
1/4 cup green pepper
1/2 cup Spanish peanuts
1 cup mayonnaise

Set overnight. When ready to serve, stir in 1 cup chow mein noodles.

Fruit Garnish

Seasonal fruit on a lettuce leaf

Dinner Rolls

2 cups flour
1/2 cup sugar
1/3 cup powdered milk
1 teaspoon salt
1 Tablespoon yeast

Mix above ingredients together with spoon.

Combine the following ingredients:

1 cup water
1 cup milk (or half-and-half)
1/3 cup Fleischmann's margarine

Microwave 1 1/2 minutes at full power. (Margarine may not be melted entirely but that's OK.) Add to dry ingredients and mix 2 minutes.

Add 3 to 3 1/2 cups more flour. (Dough should be satiny but not sticky.) Use dough hook to make rolls. Let dough rise until doubled. Punch down. Let rise until one-half doubled. Punch down. Let rest 5 minutes. Form rolls. Let double in size. Bake at 375° for 5 minutes. Turn oven down to 350° for 12 to 15 minutes (or until nicely browned).

The Nebraska Governor's Residence hosts many luncheons for civic and state organizations. Kathy Henning, the Residence's chef, bakes the rolls for all these events, as well as for dinner parties hosted by the Governor and First Lady. No matter how scrumptious the meal, it's always the rolls that get the great reviews! This dinner roll recipe is Kathy's mom's recipe, submitted by Karen Toussaint.

Complete Meals

Governor Victor Anderson had this gavel made from the spindles of the old mansion staircase.

Complete Meals

Governor's Residence
Dinner Menu:

Garden Greens Salad with Italian Dressing

Vegetable Rice Dish

Grilled Chicken Alfredo

Dinner Rolls

Apple Goodie Dessert

Garden Greens Salad with Italian Dressing

Mixed salad greens

Favorite Italian dressing is from the Olive Garden Restaurant!

Vegetable Rice Dish

1 cup jasmine rice
1 1/2 cups water with 2 Tablespoons butter

Bring water and butter to a boil. Add rice and cook 20 minutes on low heat. Turn heat off and let stand 10 minutes. (Do not stir.)

Sauté the following ingredients in butter and olive oil:

5 spears of asparagus (chopped)
2 carrots, peeled and sliced
2 celery stalks, sliced
1 green onion, sliced
Parsley

Stir vegetables into rice.

Grilled Chicken Alfredo

3 Tablespoons olive oil
2 cloves garlic, crushed

Sauté until golden but not brown.

Add 2 cups cream

Add shredded Parmesan cheese (15 to 20 ounces, depending on how thick you like it).

Heat on low until smooth. Grill chicken breast, cut into strips. Lay chicken on the rice and vegetables. Spoon Alfredo sauce over all.

Dinner Rolls

(See page 321 in the Governor's Residence Lunch Menu for recipe.)

A favorite recipe of former First Lady Stephanie Johanns, submitted by Karen Toussaint.

Apple Goodie

For apple mixture, thoroughly combine the following ingredients:

4 cups sliced apples
3/4 cup sugar
1 rounded Tablespoon flour
1/4 teaspoon salt
1 teaspoon cinnamon

For oatmeal mixture, thoroughly combine and crumb the following ingredients:

3/4 cup oatmeal
3/4 cup flour
3/4 cup light brown sugar
1/4 teaspoon soda
1/4 teaspoon baking powder
1/3 cup melted butter

Put apple mixture into baking dish. Spread oatmeal mixture over top. Bake slowly until done, 1 hour at 350°. Serve while warm with thick country cream or with ice cream. I serve this with butter brickle ice cream as a topping.

Complete Meals

Veal and Pepper with Skachooni Bread:

Veal

Peppers with Onions

Skachooni Bread

Recipes in this section were contributed by Mary Mancuso.

Ever since I can remember, our family's Christmas celebration has always been an all-day affair, lasting from just before noon on Christmas Eve until nearly midnight. My little Italian mother typically prepared elaborate meals for every holiday, but Christmas was even more so. It involved two full meals for lunch and dinner, along with an endless array of appetizers and desserts. She somehow singlehandedly fed what eventually became the thirty-plus members of our family, using the same pots and pans she had since the day she got married in a kitchen about the size of a large closet. In her

continued on page 329

Veal

2 pounds veal
Bread crumbs with Italian seasonings
4 eggs beaten in a bowl
1 cup Parmesan cheese, grated
Several fresh parsley sprigs

Bread the veal by dipping it in egg, then bread crumbs, and then grated Parmesan cheese. Place the pieces on top of one another with fresh parsley, separating each piece. It is important to use fresh parsley—besides adding flavoring, the parsley keeps the pieces from sticking to one another and will also keep the breading from separating from the meat. Place in the refrigerator for 2 hours. (The veal can be frozen at this point if you prefer to save it for a later date.)

Heat a skillet of cooking oil. Brown each piece of veal in the hot oil (parsley removed), then place in the oven at 350° for approximately 30 to 45 minutes with foil lightly covering the top. When serving, lay spoonfuls of peppers, onions, and sauce (see recipe next page) on top of the veal.

Complete Meals

Peppers with Onions

6 large green peppers
6 medium onions, sliced
2 to 3 (10-ounce) cans of tomato sauce
1 to 2 teaspoons beef bouillon, to taste

Slice the green peppers by removing the cap (stem top) and the bottom. Clean out the insides including all the seeds, then slice once lengthwise so that it will lay flat on a cookie sheet; place under the oven broiler. When the peppers begin to blister, they can be removed from the oven and placed in a brown paper sack for approximately 30 minutes. At that point, the skins can be easily peeled from the peppers. Wash them off well and then soak in cold water. Slice the peppers lengthwise into strips. (If you like, the peppers can be frozen at this point to be used another day.)

Cook onions by slightly browning them in olive oil. Place the peppers and onions together in tomato sauce. Add a little water and beef bouillon as necessary. Cook on low to medium heat uncovered for 1 hour. Be sure not to overcook or the peppers begin to dissolve.

---

continued from page 328

eighties, Mom was finally willing a few years ago to hand over the holiday celebrations to me and my siblings (and spouses, of course!). Now, each time we gather and prepare the same meals and desserts and all that goes with it, it never ceases to amaze each one of us how Mom accomplished so much with so little for so long. The noon meal for us on Christmas Eve is veal and peppers with skachooni bread. Mom's original recipe called for four bushels of peppers and ten pounds of onions. Needless to say, the serving size of this recipe needed to be pared down just a bit. And the parsley? It used to be free at the local grocery stores when Mom and the other seven Toscano brothers and sisters were growing up in

continued on page 330

continued from page 329

Little Italy in Omaha. Times have changed! But one thing hasn't changed—Mom's orders when everything's finally ready to come out of the oven: "Mangia! Mangia! But save some for everyone else!"

Mary Mancuso,
Omaha

Skachooni Bread

1 loaf of ciabatta bread, cut lengthwise
1/2 pound of butter
1/2 cup red pepper flakes
Garlic salt, to taste
1 cup grated Parmesan cheese

The name and the spelling varies widely, but *skachooni* is basically a home-made bread with a thick layer of red pepper flakes and Parmesan on top. Since most people don't have the time to bake homemade bread, just buy a large loaf of crusty bread, like ciabatta, at the store. Cut loaf in half lengthwise, lay both pieces open-faced on a cookie sheet, and brush with a bit of olive oil. Then butter the bread pieces, sprinkle garlic salt to taste, add thick layer of red pepper flakes and Parmesan to taste. Put in the oven at 375° for 5 minutes, watching it carefully so as to avoid burning it. It provides a wonderful complement to the veal and peppers.

Complete Meals

Cowboy Steak Dinner

Cowboy Steak

Rye Bread with Raspberry Jam

Waldorf Salad

Torte Dessert

Recipes in this section were contributed by Hank Edgerton.

Cowboy Steak

Salt the steak well on both sides and dredge it in flour, 2 or 3 times on each side. Heat 1 stick of butter in a large skillet, until the butter bubbles up. Slide the steak into the hot butter in one big piece. Cover and let it get hot. Turn once, cover, then repeat for both sides until each side has been on the heat twice and is nicely browned. (See The Perfectly Cooked Steak recipe, page 181.)

Rye Bread with Raspberry Jam

Waldorf Salad

Torte Dessert

4 egg whites
1 cup sugar (white)
1 cup ground graham cracker crumbs
1/2 cup coconut
1/4 cup nut meats, if desired

Beat the egg whites until stiff, and then fold in the 1 cup of sugar very slowly, gradually sprinkling it in approximately a tablespoon at a time. Add the additional ingredients. Bake in 9-inch pie pan at 350° for 30 minutes. If necessary, reduce to 300° for 10 minutes longer. Serve with whipped cream or ice cream.

Serves 6.

Complete Meals

Cheese Grits with Sandhills Trout or Glazed Salmon

Sandhills Trout

Glazed Salmon

Cheese Grits

Orzo with Spinach

Recipes in this section were contributed by Secretary of State John Gale.

While living in North Platte, Lincoln County, for twenty-nine years, I greatly enjoyed all the outdoor recreation, including hunting, fishing, canoeing, sailing, and exploring. Trout fishing in the natural, spring-fed Sandhills trout streams became a favorite pastime. Because western Nebraska sits atop the Ogallala Aquifer, fresh cold-water springs are abundant, creating many small streams that feed into many rivers, from the Niobrara to the Dismal, Elkhorn, Loup, and Cedar.

Sandhills Trout

Marinate several trout in a glass baking dish with 1 cup of lemon juice for 1 hour, turning every 15 minutes. Remove fish and clean dish. Pre-melt 1/2 inch of butter until brown in oven in baking dish. Place slivered almonds and sliced lemons inside the trout cavities for cooking. Use black pepper and fish seasoning or salt for flavor. Cook at 450° for 15 minutes until skin browns or bubbles. Baste every 3 minutes. Do not turn over. Remove and serve.

Glazed Salmon

8 ounces salmon fillet
Lemon pepper
2 teaspoons olive oil
1 Tablespoon soy sauce
2 teaspoons granular Splenda

Place salmon fillets in a heavily greased baking dish, skin side down. Season with lemon pepper to taste. Cover tightly and bake at 350° for 40 minutes. Shake together remaining ingredients to make a basting sauce. Uncover salmon and brush with the sauce. Broil until nicely browned, basting several times. We like to sprinkle it with sesame seeds and/or snipped parsley.

Complete Meals

Cheese Grits

1 1/2 cups grits
6 cups salted water
1 pound Velveeta cheese
1 1/2 sticks of butter
3 beaten eggs
11 drops of Tabasco sauce
Garlic salt

Cook the grits in the water according to the directions on the box of grits. Combine with the rest of the ingredients. Bake for 1 hour at 250° or until brown on top. Let sit for a few minutes before serving.

Makes 12 servings.

Orzo with Spinach

1/2 cup orzo
4 cups washed, ready-to-eat spinach
2 Tablespoons raisins
2 teaspoons olive oil
Salt and pepper, to taste

Place a medium saucepan three-quarters full of water over high heat. When water boils, add orzo. Cook until tender, 8 to 10 minutes. Add spinach and drain. Return to the saucepan. Stir in raisins, olive oil, salt, and pepper to taste. Sometimes we sprinkle with slivered almonds or pine nuts.

Serves 2.

On those occasions when we think we need something a little more sophisticated, we like to serve this orzo recipe with any seafood.

The kitchen has a breakfast nook area for the occasional informal meal that may take place.

Complete Meals

Harms Greek Dinner

Keftaides (Greek Meatballs)

Sanganaki (Flaming Greek Cheese)

Soupa Avgolemono (Egg and Lemon Soup)

Psomi (Continental Bread)

Salata Me Lathi Ke Lemoni
(Greek Salad with Oil and Lemon Dressing)

Kapama (Chicken with Spaghetti)

Spinach and Artichoke Casserole

Chef Lee's Bread Pudding

Recipes in this section were contributed by Senator John and Mrs. Pat Harms.

For the past ten years, we have traditionally donated a Greek dinner in honor of various community fundraising events. Two or three times a year, we typically will prepare and serve a five-course meal at our home for four to eight people. From appetizers to dessert usually takes two to two-and-a-half hours. Even though we don't have a very large Greek population in our District 48 area, the people really love Greek food. The dinners begin with five to six Greek appetizers and a dry red Greek wine. This is followed by avgolemono soup and psomi bread. The next course is Greek salad and **continued on page 339**

Keftaides (Greek Meatballs)

Combine the following ingredients and form into meatballs:

1 pound ground beef or a mixture of beef and lamb
1/2 cup fresh bread crumbs
1 teaspoon salt
1/2 cup finely chopped onion
1 Tablespoon dried parsley flakes
1/2 teaspoon garlic powder
1 teaspoon crumbled dried mint
1 egg, beaten
1/4 cup ouzo or anisette

Roll them in flour (using 1/4 cup). Place on a cookie sheet and chill for 1 hour. Heat 4 Tablespoons olive oil in a large skillet and fry the meatballs over medium-high heat until done. Serve them hot.

Makes about 32 small, appetizer-sized meatballs.

Sanganaki (Flaming Greek Cheese)

1 pound kasseri cheese
1/2 fresh lemon
2 Tablespoons warm brandy

Slice cheese into 3/4- to 1-inch slices. Place cheese in oven-proof dish. Broil approximately 3 minutes without turning. Just before serving, pour 2 Tablespoons brandy over hot cheese and ignite. Squeeze lemon over flame to extinguish. Serve hot with toasted flat-bread triangles.

Complete Meals

Soupa Avgolemono (Egg and Lemon Soup)

2 cans Swanson chicken broth
1/2 cup instant rice
4 eggs
Pepper
Lemon juice

Bring chicken broth to a boil, add rice, and cook until rice is tender. In the meantime, beat eggs until foamy, add 1 Tablespoon lemon juice and mix well. When rice is done, reduce heat. While beating the egg-and-lemon mixture, add about 1 cup of the hot broth. This will keep the eggs from curdling when added to the rest of the broth. Stir the egg mixture into the broth and continue to stir for a few minutes. Cook over very low heat for a few minutes, stirring constantly until slightly thickened. *Do not boil* as the mixture will curdle. This soup should have a distinct lemon flavor, so it is a good idea to taste it after it is heated throughout. Add more lemon juice if necessary.

continued from page 338
grilled pita bread. The main course is chicken kampama and a spinach-and-artichoke casserole, which is served with another kind of Greek wine. For dessert, a bread pudding with vanilla sauce is served along with a sweet Greek wine and coffee. Here is just a sampling of what we serve.

Complete Meals

Psomi (Continental Bread)

1/2 cup water
2 Tablespoons oil
5 Tablespoons milk
1 (1 1/4-ounce) package dry yeast
2 1/4 cups all-purpose flour
1/2 teaspoon salt
1 egg
2 Tablespoons milk
1 Tablespoon sesame seeds (optional)

Combine water, oil, and milk in a small saucepan and heat to lukewarm (105° to 115°). Pour into a small mixing bowl and dissolve the yeast in the liquids. Combine the flour and salt. Add 1 cup flour mixture and beat with an electric mixer for 2 minutes. Add the rest of the flour mixture and stir to form a stiff dough. Turn out the dough onto a floured board and knead until smooth and elastic. Place the dough in a lightly greased bowl, rotating the dough to oil the entire surface. Cover and remove to a warm place to rise until light and airy (1 to 2 hours). Punch dough down, form it into a round loaf, and place on a lightly floured cookie sheet. Beat egg with the milk and brush the loaf with this mixture. Sprinkle on sesame seeds if desired. With a very sharp knife, cut a cross on the top. Cover and allow to rise until double in size. Preheat oven to 400°. Put the bread on the middle shelf and place a small cake pan with 1 inch of hot water on the shelf beneath it. Bake for 15 minutes, then reduce the heat to 350° and bake for an additional 15 minutes. Remove from the oven and cool on a rack. Makes 1 round loaf.

Salata Me Lathi Ke Lemoni
(Greek Salad with Oil and Lemon Dressing)

Mixed salad greens
Tomatoes
Onions
Cucumbers
Kalamata olives
Feta cheese (crumbled or cubed)
Bell pepper

Tear salad greens into bite-size pieces, add remaining ingredients, and toss.
Mix 1 part lemon juice with 2 parts olive oil and pour over salad mixture.
Season to taste with salt and pepper or with a Greek seasoning such as
Cavender's All Purpose Greek Seasoning.

Kapama (Chicken with Spaghetti)

4 to 6 boneless, skinless chicken breasts
Lemon juice
Cinnamon
Oregano
Salt and pepper, to taste
Olive oil
1 medium chopped onion
1 can tomato paste
Hot water
Optional: 1/8 to 1/4 teaspoon garlic powder

Marinate breasts in lemon juice, cinnamon, salt, pepper, and oregano. (Don't be afraid to use too much cinnamon as some recipes call for 1 1/2 teaspoons.) Refrigerate breasts overnight. Next day, heat 2 Tablespoons olive oil in a heavy kettle and add chicken. Brown on both sides. Remove meat from kettle, add 1 medium chopped onion, and cook until tender. Mix 1 can tomato paste with 4 cans very hot water until sauce is smooth. Add chicken to the cooked onion. Pour the tomato sauce over the chicken to cover it. Add more sauce if necessary. Add the remaining marinade to the sauce while it is cooking. Add 1/8 to 1/4 teaspoon garlic powder if desired. Cook on medium heat until the chicken is tender. If sauce has too strong a tomato taste, add a small amount of sugar and a little more cinnamon. When chicken is done, remove from the sauce to a warm platter. Serve the sauce over spaghetti.

Complete Meals

Spinach and Artichoke Casserole

2 packages frozen chopped spinach
1 cube butter
1 onion, chopped
1 small container (8-ounces) sour cream
1/2 cup grated Parmesan cheese
1/4 teaspoon garlic salt
2 Tablespoons lemon juice
1 can artichokes, rinsed and drained well
1/2 cup Pepperidge Farm Stuffing Mix

Cook spinach and drain well. Set aside. Sauté onion in butter and remove from heat. Add spinach and remaining ingredients except artichokes and stuffing mix. Mix well. Slice artichokes and put in bottom of a 1-quart greased casserole dish. Spoon mixture over artichokes and sprinkle with stuffing mix. Bake uncovered at 350° for 30 minutes.

Chef Lee's Bread Pudding

3 eggs, beaten
2 Tablespoons brown sugar
1/2 teaspoon nutmeg
3 cups heavy cream
4 cups cubed, day-old white bread
1 1/2 cups sugar
1 Tablespoon vanilla
1/2 stick butter, melted
Dash of yellow food coloring (optional)
3/4 cup raisins

Combine eggs, sugars, vanilla, and nutmeg. Add melted butter, then cream, then food coloring, and mix well. Stir in cubed bread and raisins and let stand 10 to 15 minutes. Pour into well-greased deep pan or casserole. Bake at 375° for 45 to 60 minutes until golden brown. Serve warm, topped with Butter Vanilla Sauce (below).

Serves 6 to 8.

Butter Vanilla Sauce

1 beaten egg
1/2 cup white sugar
1 Tablespoon flour
Dash of nutmeg
3 Tablespoons brown sugar
2 Tablespoons butter, melted

1 teaspoon vanilla
1 1/4 cups heavy cream

Combine in the top of a double boiler. Cook, stirring until thickened.

In August 2007 the fiftieth anniversary of the present Governor's Residence was oberved with tours and special events hosted by Governor Dave Heineman and First Lady Sally Ganem. In 2008 the Nebraska Governor's Residence was listed in the National Register of Historic Places.

346

Acknowledgements

We gratefully acknowledge the contributions and support of the following individuals and organizations.

Cookbook Committee

Brenda Decker
Nancy Enstrom
Carol Gale
Sally Ganem
Jeff Jensen
Jill Karpisek
Wilma L. Lorenz
Sharon Ann Louden
Mary Mancuso
Kerstin O'Connor
Jane Oligmueller
Karen Toussaint
Jolene Ward
Anita Wiechman

Sponsors

Acklie Charitable Foundation
Dean and Gaylene Aden

Tam and Kathleen Allan
Aquila, Inc.
Dwayne Brown
B/D Construction
Brunswick State Bank
Burlington Northern Trust
Cash-Wa Distributing Co.
Cattlemen's Association
Cornerstone Bank
Cornhusker Republican Womens Club
Countryside Bank
Chris M. Dibbern and Michael B. Hybl
The First National Bank, Valentine, Nebraska
First National Bank of Wayne
First State Bank & Trust Company
FirsTier Bank
Fremont Beef Company
Fremont National Bank & Trust Company
First Lady Sally Ganem and Governor Dave Heineman
Gappa Distributing Inc.
Betty Henning
Thomas J. and Mary E. Henning
Kelly and Virginia Holthus
Infusionmedia Publishing Inc.
Inner-Motion, Inc.
IntelliCom Computer Consulting, Inc.
Brad Kernick
Gene and Connie Koepke
Lincoln Electric System
Lovgren Marketing
Norris and Lori Marshall

348   *Acknowledgements*

John and Nancy McCoy
Morris Printing Group, Inc.
Kenneth Morrison
Nebraska Pork Producers Association, Inc.
Nebraska Poultry Industries, Inc.
Nebraskaland Foundation Inc.
Oak Creek Valley Bank
Prairie Fire Newspaper
J. Peter Ricketts
Robert and Janice Batt Foundation
Royal Forwarding, Inc.
Rupert Dunklau Foundation, Inc.
Rural Electric Association
Sahling Kenworth, Inc.
James and Kelly Jo Shada
Simon Family Donor-Advised Fund
SourceGas
TierOne Charitable Foundation
Tyson Foods, Inc.
William and Linda Vosik
Wiechman Pig Co., Inc.
Michael B. and Gail Yanney
Paul and Linda Younes

Index

Appetizers & Beverages 13

Baked Gizzards 15

Crabmeat Mold 16

Mom's Yummy Cheese Ball 16

Cheese Crisps 17

German Cheese Spread 17

Beef and Cheese Ball 18

Cowboy Caviar 19

Reuben Balls 20

Garlic Dip 21

Scooper Beef 22

Chicken Enchilada Dip 23

Sunflower Seed Dip 24

Marinated Eggplant, Italian Melanzane Marinate 25

Garlic Marinated Mushrooms 26

English Olive Appetizers 26

Mushroom Croustades 27

Stuffed Baby Baked Potatoes 28

Hanky Panky 29

Tomato and Basil Appetizer 30

Cranberry Roll-Ups 30

Caramel Apple Cones 31

Spiced Candied Walnuts 32

Sugared Pecans 33

Vodka and Citrus Cured Salmon 34

Best Holiday Fish 35

Poor Man's Cappuccino Mix 36

Summer Punch 37

Cranberry-Apple Punch 38
Mock Champagne 39
Sweet Almond Tea 40
Mock Sangria 41

Breads & Rolls 43

Cinnamon Rolls 45
Swedish Coffee Bread 46
Kolache 47
Kolace 49
Kolac Cheese Bread 51
Butterscotch Rolls 52
Prize Roll Recipe 53
Grandma Pewee's Dinner Rolls 54
Garlic Monkey Bread 55
Lithuanian Bacon Buns 56
Coffee Cake 57
SAL's Gumdrop Bread 58
Mom Nelson's Banana Bread 59
Zucchini Bread 60
Triple Berry Muffins 61
Oat Bran Blueberry Muffins 62
Apple-Butterscotch Muffins 63
Six Weeks Raisin Bran Muffins 64
Ingrid's Pepparkaka (Spice Cake) 65
Baking Powder Biscuits 66
Sourdough Biscuit 67
Connie's 'Red Lobster' Cheese Garlic Biscuits 68
Corn Bread Jenn 69
Easy Buckwheat Flapjacks 70
Joel's Cornmeal Pancakes 71

Index   351

Bede's Favorite Pancakes 72
Ultimate Pancakes and Waffles 72
Aebelskiver 73
Grandma Cody's Doughnuts 74
German Zwieback 75
Mom's Knäckerbröd (Swedish Hardtack) 76

Cakes, Cookies & Candy 257

Angel-Food Cake 259
Coconut Cake 260
Sourdough Chocolate Cake 261
Lady Baltimore Cake 262
Italian Prune Cake 264
Chocolate Zucchini Cake 265
Chocolate Chip Zucchini Cake 266
Karithopita (Walnut Cake) 267
Applesauce Cake 268
Best Chocolate Cake 269
Waldorf-Astoria Red Velvet Cake 270
Carrot Cake 271
Les Gateaux 272
Chocolate Chip Oatmeal Cookies (Famous FHS Pressbox Cookies) 273
M&M Coconut Macaroon Cookies 274
Candy Bar Cookies 275
Mexican Wedding Cookies (Cuernitos) 276
Oatmeal Cranberry White Chocolate Chunk Cookies 277
Senator Howard's Lace Cookies 278
Drop Sugar Cookies 279
Anise Cookies 280
Chocolate Chip Oatmeal Cookies 281
Grandma O's White Crisp Cookies 282

Index

Pumpkin Chocolate Chip Cookies 283

Danish Sugar Cookies 284

Sugar Cookies 285

Lemon Crisscross Cookies 286

Mrs. Heine's Oatmeal Raisin Cookies 287

Frosted Rhubarb Cookies 288

Gingersnaps 289

Peppernuts 290

Salted Nut Roll 291

Peanut Butter Balls 291

Janie's Fudge 292

Peanut Butter Fantasy Fudge 294

Pralines 295

Complete Meals 313

Governor's Residence Breakfast Menu 315

Homestyle Good Morning Casserole 316

Bran Muffins 317

Governor's Residence Lunch Menu 319

Chicken Salad 320

Fruit Garnish 320

Dinner Rolls 321

Governor's Residence Dinner Menu 323

Garden Greens Salad with Italian Dressing 324

Vegetable Rice Dish 324

Grilled Chicken Alfredo 325

Dinner Rolls 325 (recipe page 321)

Apple Goodie 326

Veal and Pepper with Skachooni Bread 327

Veal 328

Peppers with Onions 329

Index   353

Skachooni Bread 330

Cowboy Steak Dinner 331

Cowboy Steak 332

Rye Bread with Raspberry Jam 332

Waldorf Salad 332

Torte Dessert 332

Cheese Grits with Sandhills Trout or Glazed Salmon 333

Sandhills Trout 334

Glazed Salmon 334

Cheese Grits 335

Orzo with Spinach 335

Harms Greek Dinner 337

Keftaides (Greek Meatballs) 338

Sanganaki (Flaming Greek Cheese) 338

Soupa Avgolemono (Egg and Lemon Soup) 339

Psomi (Continental Bread) 340

Salata Me Lathi Ke Lemoni (Greek Salad with Oil and Lemon Dressing) 341

Kapama (Chicken with Spaghetti) 342

Spinach and Artichoke Casserole 343

Chef Lee's Bread Pudding 344

Governor & First Lady Recipes 1

Stuffed Grape Leaves 3

Tabbouleh 5

Sally's Favorite Salad Dressing 6

Green Beans with a Mediterranean Twist 7

Middle Eastern Lemonade 8

The 'Gov' Burger 9

Creamed Corn 10

Main Dishes & Casseroles 121

Tastees 123

Election Joes 124

Pizza Burgers 125

Mexican Casserole 126

Taco Casserole 127

Zucchini-Hamburger Casserole 128

Overnight Casserole 129

Cabbage Casserole 130

German Skillet Dinner 131

Tenderloin and Wild Rice Casserole 132

Pork Steak and Sauerkraut 133

Flishcky (Czechoslovakian Casserole) 134

Nelson's Creek Noodle Tuna Casserole 135

Pheasant Dressing Casserole 136

Creamed Chicken 137

Mexican Chicken 138

Chicken Soufflé 139

Grilled Chicken Fettuccine with Sun-Dried Tomatoes 140

Easy Chicken/Stuffing Casserole 142

Brunch Pizza Squares 143

Ziploc Omelet 144

Sausage, Egg and Cheese Casserole 145

Breakfast Casserole 147

Senator's Favorite Breakfast Casserole 148

Brunch Enchiladas 149

Bread/Cheese Soufflé 150

Cheese and Tomato Salad Pizza 151

Nana's Pizza Topping Sauce 153

Pop Over Pizza 154

Pizza Spaghetti 155

Index   355

Lasagna 156

'No Peek' Spaghetti 157

Fabulous Zucchini Pie 158

Eggplant Sicilian Caponata 159

Summer Squash or Zucchini Casserole 160

Vegetable Casserole Delight 161

Potato Dressing 162

Scotch-Currant Dressing 163

Knip 164

Meat, Poultry & Seafood 167

Beef Fillet with Madeira Sauce 169

Boeuf Bourguignon 171

Omaha Steaks Famous Grilled Peppered Filet Mignon 174

Standing Rib Roast 175

Baked Steak 176

Zobel's Café German Steak 177

Swiss Steak 178

Jan's 'Famous Dave's' Baby Back Ribs 180

The Perfectly Cooked Steak 181

Barbecued Beef 182

Rouladen und Sosse (Rolled and Stuffed Braised Beef) 183

Sweet and Sour Meatballs 185

Swedish Meatballs 186

Aunt Tina's Meatballs 187

Meatballs with Sauce 188

Italian Meatballs 189

Company Meatloaf 190

Best-Ever Meatloaf 191

Frikadeller (Danish Meat Patties) 192

Cajun Burgers 193

Mediterranean Lamb Shanks 194

Veal Oscar 195

Ham Balls 196

Pork Chili 197

Sun-Dried Tomato Pesto Stuffed Pork 198

Artichoke-Chicken Mélange 199

Chicken Piccata 200

Sunlight Chicken 201

Grilled Chicken Cordon Bleu 202

Oven-Baked Herb-Crusted Chicken 203

Baked Halibut 204

Fish in Salsa Sauce 204

Baked Stuffed Shrimp 205

Shrimp and Tortellini 206

Seafood Strudel 207

Pies, Pastries & Desserts 211

Amy's Cheesecake 213

Orange Almond Biscotti 215

Gene Autry's Peanut Butter Pie 217

'Hilltop Café' Pie Crust 218

Mabel's Shoofly Pie 219

Mom's Favorite Sour Cream Raisin Pie 220

Pineapple-Rhubarb Pie 221

Plain-Jane Apple Pie 222

Reka's Mincemeat Pie 223

Strawberry-Rhubarb Pie 224

Watermelon Pie 225

Extra-Special Apple Crisp 226

My Apple Cobbler 227

Apple Strudel 228

Index

Peach Cobbler 229

Swedish Tea Logs 230

Peanut Butter Mud Bars 232

Prize-Winning Lemon Squares 234

Treasure Bars 235

Rhubarb Bars 236

Danish Apple Bars 237

Easy Brownies ... To Knock Your Socks Off! 238

Scandinavian Almond Bars 239

Chocolate Franges 241

Caramel Apple Cheesecake 242

Herb's Vanilla Ice Cream 244

Ice Cream Sandwich Dessert 244

Mexican Fried Ice Cream (Without Frying) 245

Listy (Leaves) 245

Cranberry Dessert 246

Chocolate Bread Pudding 247

Grandma Hannah's Bread Pudding 248

Cottage Cheese Varenikje 249

Harriet's Swedish Rice Pudding 251

Maybiddle Pudding 252

Christmas Plum Pudding 253

Ostkaka (Swedish Custard) 254

Hot Fruit Casserole 255

Soups, Salads & Vegetables 79

Jim's Chili 81

Easy Gourmet Vegetable Beef Soup 82

German Noodles and Butterballs Soup 83

Fruit Soup 84

Spicy Potato Soup 85

Boys Town Butternut Squash and Apple Soup 86

Homemade Tomato Soup 88

Chili Soup 89

Norma's White Chili 90

Halibut Chowder 91

Seafood Chowder 92

Hearty Beef and Sausage Stew 93

Bigos (Traditional Hunter's Stew) 94

Mulligan Stew 95

Nebraska-Style Fruit Salad 96

Broccoli Slaw 97

Black Bean Shrimp Salad 98

Festive Tossed Salad 99

Chicken Salad 100

Taffy Apple Salad 101

Strawberry Nut Salad 102

Cauliflower and Broccoli Salad 103

Green Stuff 104

Tim's Potato Salad 105

Walnut Tuna Salad 106

BLT Macaroni Salad 107

Andrea's Branding Taco Salad 108

Perfection Salad 109

Romaine and Artichoke Salad 110

Chinese Chicken Toss 111

Creamed Green Beans with Onions 112

Eggplant Gratin 113

Potatoes Florentine 114

Harvest Squash 115

Crunchy Potato Balls 116

Potato Dumplings 117

Index 359

Aunt Anna's Baked Beans 118
Pear Salad with Gorgonzola Dressing 119

This & That 297

Pinezucot Jam or Cranzu-Raspberry Jam 299
Jalapeño Hot Pepper Jelly 300
Ice Cream Topping 301
Grandma Katie's Hot Mustard 302
Honey and Oats Granola 303
Homemade Noodles 304
Grandma's Noodles 305
Sourdough Starter 306
Sweet and Tangy Meat Sauce 307
Just Like Dorothy Lynch Dressing 308
Favorite Salad Dressing 309
Poppy Seed Dressing 310
Mock Olive Garden Dressing 310

Inspired Recipes from Nebraska

Please reserve _____ copies of *Inspired Recipes from Nebraska* at $29.95 each for me.

Nebraska residents please add $2.10 sales tax to each book. Plus $4.00 shipping and handling per book.

TOTAL AMOUNT: _____

PLEASE SHIP TO

Name: _____

Address: _____

City/State/ZIP: _____

Phone: _____

E-mail: _____

Payment must accompany order. We accept checks and money orders.

Friends of the Governor's Residence
Nebraska Community Foundation, 650 J St., Lincoln, NE 68508
Proceeds will be used to fund updating and upgrading of the Nebraska Governor's Residence.

- -

Inspired Recipes from Nebraska

Please reserve _____ copies of *Inspired Recipes from Nebraska* at $29.95 each for me.

Nebraska residents please add $2.10 sales tax to each book. Plus $4.00 shipping and handling per book.

TOTAL AMOUNT: _____

PLEASE SHIP TO

Name: _____

Address: _____

City/State/ZIP: _____

Phone: _____

E-mail: _____

Payment must accompany order. We accept checks and money orders.

Friends of the Governor's Residence
Nebraska Community Foundation, 650 J St., Lincoln, NE 68508
Proceeds will be used to fund updating and upgrading of the Nebraska Governor's Residence.